COMM

To Nick,
May God bless you always

A. Miller

Committed

Anthony Millen

InsideOut **Publications**
EDMONTON
LONDON

Copyright © Anthony Millen 2000

The right of Anthony Millen to be identified as author of this book has been asserted by him in accordance with the Copyright, Designs and Patents Act 1988.

First published 2000

Published by: ***InsideOut*** Publications
P.O. Box 17647
Edmonton
London N9 9WT

ISBN   0-9539431-0-0

All rights reserved.
No part of this publication may be reproduced or transmitted in any form or by any means, electronic or mechanical, including photocopy, recording, or any information storage and retrieval system, without permission in writing from the publisher.

Scripture quotations taken from the Holy Bible, New International Version, copyright © 1973, 1978, 1984 by the International Bible Society. Used by permission.

Extracts from the Authorized Version of the Bible (The King James Bible), the rights in which are vested in the Crown, are reproduced by permission of the Crown's Patentee, Cambridge University Press.

Designed and produced by
Bookprint Creative Services
P.O. Box 827, BN21 3YJ, England

Printed in Great Britain

Acknowledgements

My sincere thanks to all my family who were caught up in this long running saga. To Cheryl, my darling wife, who came week after week to visit me, for her typing of the scripts and providing much of the material in this book.

To all those many people in Prison and outside who believed me to be innocent; who gave of their time and money, but above all their encouragement and prayers.

To all those who worked so very hard for the "Free Anthony Millen Campaign".

To all those members of my church who supported me throughout the long dark days.

To Sue Hunter for editing the script; and Bob Hunter who encouraged me to write this book and undertook the typesetting.

Anthony Millen

I warmly dedicate this book to

Cheryl

*the most wonderful, courageous
and remarkable woman
I have ever met.*

Contents

	Foreword	9
1.	The Ackees Affair	11
2.	The Nightmare	16
3.	Inside Out	26
4.	The Time in Between	32
5.	Setting Up the Business	36
6.	The Fateful Trip	39
7.	The Trial	46
8.	From Pulpit to Prison	52
9.	My Name and My Roots	56
10.	Faith on Trial	65
11.	Through the Fire - Bullingdon	75
12.	My Appeal to Justice	87
13.	Preacher Man at The Mount	91
14.	Living on a Knife Edge - Latchmere House	102
15.	Cheryl's Story	110
16.	Free to Serve	120
	Bible References	124

Foreword

I am very pleased to have this opportunity to lend my support to the publication of this book. During the last eight years my wife, Mary, and I have had the privilege to work for 'Within the Walls' inside British Prisons. Our work has had the full support of the Chaplain General.

During our visits to prisons and whilst speaking with the men, we heard of Anthony Millen and the work being done from his cell and in the various prison chapels. We met him only briefly in HMP Bullingdon, as he was leaving for HMP The Mount. His reputation for integrity and fearless speaking of the love and saving power of Jesus Christ was clear from the men with whom he had come in close contact.

Anthony, 'Tony' to his friends and other prisoners, was always ready to stop and help men in need. In this book you will read of personal encounters of people who came face to face with Jesus at times of great crisis. You will read of their changed lives, and even the reconciliation of these inmates to their wives and loved ones. Those whom Tony came in contact with could never be the same again. He gives complete glory to God for what he endured and the changed lives of many people.

This book will be a blessing to people who find themselves caught up in troubles not of their making. You will learn of a christian family supporting their loved one through the dark days and on into the light. To men held in detention, with long sentences, the reading of this book will bring hope and a new life.

I strongly recommend this book; read it and pass it on.

Willie Bell

Evangelist, 'Within the Walls'.
Leeds United, Scottish Internationalist
and former Birmingham City Football Manager.

****

This is an accurate account of events as far as my memory serves me. However, some names and identities have been changed, to protect the innocent.
I would not wish anyone else to suffer from false accusations, as I have done.

****

1

The Ackees Affair

I shall never be able to forget 11th March 1992. However long I live, and whatever I manage to do with the rest of my life, that one day will always remain clearly imprinted on my mind. It had started off quite normally, I remember. It was a Wednesday, and very cold when I got up early to begin the day's work. I had arranged to meet Ralph, my business partner, at the warehouse in Tottenham. We had each planned to bring a friend to help with the unloading of our consignment of goods from my home-country, Jamaica. Ralph and I had invested our redundancy money some six months earlier in the business of importing Jamaican foodstuffs into London to be sold in the small West Indian outlets in our area. We had had plenty of encouragement from shopkeepers, and it looked like we were going to make a go of it. This was the third consignment we had taken delivery of.

It was 6.00 a.m. when James and I met Ralph and Len outside the warehouse.

"Did you get here earlier?" queried Ralph.

"No, why?" I asked.

"The gate and the door are both unlocked. I thought you said we would have to do that."

"Well," I said, "It might have been one of the other workers on the premises. Never mind, let's get on with it. Any sign of the container?"

"Is that it?" called James, as a lorry with a container went past in the other direction. It certainly looked like what we were waiting for, so it was a relief when a bit later it came in sight again and this time drew up beside us. There were two men in the cab and the driver's mate leaped out almost before the lorry stopped.

"Hold it you guys!" he yelled urgently "Don't touch that!"

I couldn't see what he was making such a fuss about; there seemed to be a wire on the trailer unit he didn't want us to touch. We were far more concerned about the goods, and I started to break the seal on the container unit. I couldn't break it very easily, so I went off to my van and returned with a hammer.

As soon as we had access to our goods, the driver's mate went off to get some breakfast and we climbed into the container.

"Right boys!" I said, "Pass these along the line there."

We all formed a chain and I began passing out the goods to Len, who passed them to James, and Ralph stacked them in the unit. Pretty soon I came across two boxes of fruit drink samples I had ordered.

"Put these to one side, Ralph; we'll need some refreshment before we've finished."

At this point Len jumped up into the container beside me.

"I can see you're getting tired Brother T. I'll give you a hand."

Together we passed out about eighty cartons, and I was really flagging. Even so, I wasn't too tired to notice that one carton was not properly sealed; when I checked inside I found there was a tin missing.

"Something funny here, Ralph!" I yelled. "Put it to one side. Hey, just a minute! this one's light, and this one."

There was nothing for it, I had to stop unloading and investigate. I opened one of the boxes and found it full of tins labelled Eve; this was totally different from the green and yellow ackees (a popular West Indian fruit) which I had ordered. When I looked closer at the tins I found that several of them were empty.

"Typical Jamaicans," James quipped, "they ate out the ackees and sent us the empty tins."

We all started laughing; it wasn't so much what he said, but how he said it. We all knew it was no laughing matter. I guessed something had gone seriously wrong at the canning factory. We would have to stack all the questionable boxes separately from the others, and it would mean I would have to return them to the shipping agents and insist on my money back from the factory of origin in Jamaica. It looked as though this shipment was going to be nowhere near as plain sailing as the previous two.

"OK Ralph," I sighed, "I'll carry on with this for now."

Nearly two hours had passed and I knew he needed to get off to his job. After we had finished, it appeared that the lorry driver's mate was getting rather anxious. The driver had tried to move off, but found the entrance to the yard blocked by another vehicle.

"Can you go round the corner and ask the police to move the car for me?" he asked.

It didn't take a moment for me to nip round the corner to the police station. Soon the problem was sorted out and the lorry disappeared, leaving us with our dud boxes still stacked in the yard, only a few feet from the main road. When we looked closely at them we found that several of the tins had been opened and the lids stuck on again. To my astonishment I saw clear traces of soup and baked beans inside some of the tins! These tins had been opened, the food taken out, the labels torn off and replaced by ackees labels. It didn't make any sort of sense, but it was clear that we had a major problem on our hands and we weren't going to be able to sort it out now. I needed to go home, phone the factory and query the whole shipment. Anyhow, I'd promised my wife, Cheryl, that I'd be back home by 8.30 a.m.

"Here, have one of these Jim. You've earned it. You too Len."

The three of us each had one of the sample drinks; we then bent our heads in prayer, thanking God for the safe arrival of the container. That ordinary act was to go against me later, but to us, it was just a natural and everyday thing to pray about the smallest details of our lives.

"Come on you two, I'll give you a lift. Just let me lock up."

We walked out in single file, but our path was blocked by two men I didn't recognise; one was short and stocky, the other was tall with ginger hair. I looked up and suddenly realised that the gate to the warehouse was surrounded by cars, and men on foot. They hadn't been there before; they must have arrived while I was locking up. They must have been watching us. I felt a sudden chill of fear and incomprehension.

"What's going on?" I asked.

"Are you Anthony Millen?" queried the tall guy. I agreed, wondering who he was.

"I have to arrest you under suspicion of importing drugs."

What! I couldn't understand what this fellow was talking about. Me? a respected family man, a pillar of the church and of my local community, this couldn't be real. I looked at James's face, and Len's, expecting to see the familiar grins; maybe this was a Jeremy Beadle type joke. But no, they looked as stunned and uncomprehending as I felt. I tried to speak to James, but several of the men prevented me. I guess they must have identified themselves to us as plain clothes police officers, but I was too shocked to take it in properly. The chap stood there, insistent, but unhurried. I groped round in my mind for a possible clue as to what he could be talking about, and suddenly thought of those empty, glued up tins which I didn't recognise and certainly hadn't ordered. I asked him bluntly if there had been drugs in the container.

"Something like that," he agreed, without a trace of emotion. "Hold out your arms." Handcuffs were slapped tightly on my wrists. I looked across and saw that the same thing was happening to the other two.

"Jim....!" I began desperately.

"Shut up," one of the officers interrupted curtly. "There's to be no communication, no talking between yourselves. You come with me."

We were all taken in separate cars to Customs House.

The nightmare had begun.

2

The Nightmare

We were driven separately to Customs House, a journey of about fifteen miles. I sat alone, handcuffed, in the back of the car. The two officers sat in the front. It was a bewildering journey. By then I realised the officers were Customs Police; they were talking to me about cricket of all things. I guess they were trying to put my mind at ease, but it wasn't helping. So many things were buzzing through my head that I couldn't think clearly. I thought of my dilemma over and over. I hadn't seen any drugs; and if there were any, how did they get into the container? There must have been a mistake. Who could have put them there, and why? Did they suspect that I was involved in a crime? I felt gutted, but felt sure that they would see I was an innocent man and send me home.

Customs House was in the City of London. It struck me as a cold, bleak building with very few windows, which meant the lights were on most of the time. When we arrived I was taken down many different corridors and up some flights of stairs until we arrived at a small reception area.

"Your name?" a stern-faced, dark haired woman officer demanded.

"Anthony Millen."

"Do you have the name of a solicitor I can contact for you?" she asked.

"I don't need a solicitor," I replied very firmly. "I've done nothing wrong. This is all some terrible mistake." She didn't even raise her head,

"Don't worry," she said, "I'll get one off the list for you." She carried on writing while the two officers standing with me took off my handcuffs and told me to empty my pockets.

"Right, along here," one of them said as they escorted me down the corridor to a huge cell, empty, apart from the toilet and a long wooden bench covered with a mat.

All sorts of questions raced through my mind again as I sat in the cell overlooking the River Thames. I remember how cold it was and I thought of my family and home. What would Cheryl, my wife, be thinking when I didn't return home at the agreed time? Would she go and look for me at the warehouse? If so, she would find my yellow van parked outside and maybe realise something was wrong. I had had to hand in all my keys; would they go to our home? Supposing Cheryl returned and found customs officers there? I thought too of my church and wondered what their re-action would be when they heard the news. I thought of Ralph and the others and suddenly a feeling of fear crept over me as I wondered what was going to happen next. It was total disbelief - a devilish nightmare - surely I would wake up any moment now. To my dismay it was all real. If I was innocent and felt like this, how does someone feel if he is guilty?

"You all right Millen, are you being treated OK?" a man asked as he put his head into my cell. "It shouldn't take much longer now." The first time that happened I felt enormously relieved; I really believed that I was going to be let out at any moment, and my hopes soared. But all through that long, confusing day officers kept popping into my cell, checking to see if I was alright, and still nothing was explained to me.

I was allowed a very brief phone-call with Cheryl, but we were both too numb to say much. I could tell she was close to tears, and that she knew that I was, too. Neither of us could understand exactly what was happening, so we could only try to re-assure each other that it must be some dreadful mistake and that we would just have to wait until it was sorted out. I knew it must have been as difficult for Cheryl, at home on her own as it was for me, locked up in this strange place. But it was a long time before I managed to piece together the details of how her ordeal had started.

When I did not arrive home at 8.30 a.m. as I had promised, she had waited over an hour and then made her way to the warehouse to see where I was. As I guessed, she had seen my van parked outside, looked inside and noticed that the glove compartment was open and papers scattered around. She peered in the window of the warehouse unit and saw that my goods had arrived from Jamaica, but she could see no sign of me. She drove around looking for me for half an hour then decided to go home to see if I had phoned and left a message on the answering machine.

By the time she got home she was pretty worried and didn't even look at the piece of paper lying on the mat; she just picked it up and made straight for the answering machine. The light on it was flashing, but she couldn't get it to work. So she opened it up and found that the tape was missing. That didn't make any sense - she knew there had been one there when she went out. She sat down, totally confused, and glanced at the sheet of paper which was still in her hand. She was horrified to read that while she had been out looking for me, the house had been searched by Customs Police. Immediately she phoned the number on the paper and asked what was going on. Poor Cheryl; she was told coldly, and without warning, that I had been arrested on suspicion of importing drugs.

"That's not possible!" was her immediate re-action, "We're not that sort of people! You must have made a mistake!" But the voice on the line was disinterested, and simply told her she could speak to me for a brief moment, if she wanted. I couldn't say anything to re-assure her, and I was unaware that when she put the phone down and looked round the room she noticed that certain items were not as she had left them. Still in a state of shock, she went through the house to see exactly what had been disturbed, and realised that they had searched the whole place, from the bedrooms right down to the cellar. Cheryl felt sick inside at this totally unexpected invasion of our privacy but she began to hope that, as they couldn't have found anything, they would soon release me.

Miles away from her, I also hoped that with no evidence against me, I would soon be free. When the meal of cold pie and beans arrived, I didn't eat it; I did not want to spoil my appetite for dinner at home that evening!

I waited hopefully, and was relieved when at last I heard footsteps again stopping outside my door.

"Here's a towel for you, Millen," said an officer I hadn't seen before, "and some soap. I'll need to stand by while you have a shower."

"What do I want them for?" I asked, in genuine bewilderment, "I'll get a shower as soon as I get home tonight."

"You're not going anywhere tonight, Millen, you might as well get used to the idea."

"I don't understand this," I said firmly. "I can answer every question they ask me. I'll tell them the absolute truth. I know I'm innocent of any crime, so how can I be kept here?"

"Well mate," he replied "It seems that not everyone here is as convinced of your innocence as you are. So you might as well get your shower." I needed a shower, but I felt humiliated and degraded as I took it, with the door open. Apart from stripping off before doctors, I had never been in that position before. I resented the indignity of using other people's towels. I passed James and Len as I went to the shower, but I was not allowed to talk to them, or find out how they were coping with the situation. James tried to speak to me, but was quickly told to shut up.

It must have been about six o'clock in the evening when the two officers who had escorted me to Customs House came into the room.

"This way Millen," one of them said, as they took me into an interrogation room. "This is the solicitor who has been appointed to represent you." He indicated a woman already sitting in the room, and I realised they had been waiting for her to arrive before they could question me. The questions started immediately.

"Now, first of all, can you tell us who helped you pack your container, in Jamaica?" I quickly gave the name of the person I had left in charge of the packing, Winston Browne. Answering the questions was not a problem to me, because I was simply reporting the facts.

"Where did you buy the goods?"

"From various canning factories in Jamaica."

"How many shipments had you previously made?"

"Two."

"Give us the names of the people who helped you."

Again I repeated the name, Winston Browne, an old family friend. They kept asking me the same questions over and over from different angles. Patiently I kept replying; telling the truth, and nothing but the truth. Soon they would see I was an innocent man.

The solicitor said nothing until towards the end of the interview when one of the Customs officers asked me to sign a paper to say that the drugs which had allegedly been in my container could be destroyed. I felt totally confused. I didn't know anything about any drugs, so how could I sign to say I gave permission for them to be destroyed.

"Can I see the drugs first?" I asked. I didn't really know what to say. Both Customs officers immediately said that would be too difficult; quite impossible; out of the question. They definitely wanted this paper dealt with. I still didn't want to sign anything at this stage. Desperately I looked round the room, trying to think what I should do, looking for some-one to advise me. The solicitor indicated to me that I should sign; that it would be OK for me to do so.

Naively, I signed.

"OK. Back to your cell now," one of the officers said, as I was escorted back after the lengthy interrogation.

That night I prayed earnestly that God would allow these people to see the innocence in the four of us and allow us to go home. I hardly slept at all. I had expected to be safely at home with my family by then, and I knew my young children would have been devastated when I did not go home that night. I wondered why I was there and how long I would have to stay there. I realised how serious the situation was when I was told I had to be further interrogated. What if there really had been drugs in those mysterious tins? My heart went cold. I couldn't understand how they could have got there, or who would have put them there, or why. Maybe some-one had planted them? Perhaps it was a rival trading company, envious of our new-found success. Or perhaps it was a trumped up charge; but for what reason? and why me?

In the morning the full horror of my situation came flooding back. There were more questions.

"When did you go to Jamaica?"

"How much did you pay for the drugs?"

"Where did you get the money to pay for the drugs?"

The questions went on and on, but I had nothing to hide. I answered each one as straightforwardly as possible; then they locked me up again. Most of the day was spent in interrogation. I asked myself why they thought I had done something wrong. I couldn't understand it at all. I spent the whole afternoon going over my predicament.

In the evening another two officers came to my cell and read to me from a sheet of paper.

"Anthony Millen, you are charged for Being Knowingly Concerned in the Importation of Drugs into the UK on 11th March, 1992, and you will appear before the Magistrates Court in the morning."

My heart pounded faster and faster, fear gripped my stomach and coldness swept over my body. I looked at them with a blank expression and total disbelief. They had actually charged me. I had been charged for a crime I knew nothing about. At this time there was nothing anyone could say to comfort me.

They told me that I would be taken to Ipswich and from there to the Magistrates Court at Felixstowe, where our shipment had entered the country. I asked if I could see my wife before I was taken from London; but this was refused. I asked if I could speak to the others. I knew that Ralph must also have been brought in, as I had heard his unmistakable voice questioning his predicament and not understanding. I felt so sorry for him. He was a kind and gentle man, and this harshness could break him. We were not allowed to speak together, and had to travel separately to Ipswich.

That night I was taken something like 70 miles, handcuffed, in the back of a car to a police cell in Ipswich. My mind was racing nineteen to the dozen. I was mentally and physically worn out, yet sleep had disappeared from my eyes. I felt dirty and needed a good bath. I just couldn't fathom out what was happening to me. It was still all a daze, a nightmare. A horror of great darkness, it seemed, had fallen on me. I was so confused. I had told them everything I knew and they didn't believe me. How could they charge me without evidence? There were no drugs to be seen on the container. All I could think of was that I was innocent. So many times you hear about miscarriages of justice and so many people in prison innocently. Now it seemed it was happening to me.

We arrived at the police station at Ipswich and then I saw Ralph and the others. Ralph and I were put into the same cell and James and Len were put into another. Fear had taken hold of Ralph - especially in the stomach area. I felt so very sorry for him. Here was an innocent man who had never been in trouble with the police after nearly 40 years in this country. We prayed together and I tried to comfort him the best I could, but nothing seemed to help.

Ipswich police station was unbearably hot. The central heating must have been full on, and there was no visible ventilation. In our cell there was one wooden bench with a foam mat on it for us to sleep on, so we had to lie down "head to tail". But we couldn't sleep, although we tried. Ralph was moaning in pain with his stomach upset and in the next cell there was a woman crying uncontrollably. She cried the whole night and none of the officers would take any notice of her.

"Let me out! I want to go home," she kept on shouting.

"Shut up! you crazy idiot," yelled a man in a neighbouring cell, "where do you think the rest of us want to go?" The slanging match kept on and on. Now and then I would have flashbacks of my home and wondered how Cheryl and the children were coping. At some point I must have dozed off, only to be awakened again by the woman. It seemed as if the devil had placed her next door to us to add to the torture we were going through.

Next morning the cell door opened and we were given something that resembled breakfast. Then we were allowed to wash and shave. We were taken to another room to be fingerprinted and photographed. Before long we were on our way to Felixstowe.

We reached Felixstowe police station where our families had arrived with a change of clothing. I was able to speak briefly with Cheryl. The officers relented and gave us about five minutes together. It was so good to see her, but there wasn't much we could say, with the police officers standing there. It must have been heartbreaking for our families to have to travel such a long distance from London to Felixstowe knowing that we had been charged for Importing Drugs.

The four of us were taken handcuffed to Felixstowe Magistrates Court. In the court I was amazed to see the man who had sat beside the driver of the container lorry on Wednesday. I later realised that he was a plain clothes Customs officer; that probably explained how he knew exactly where the local police station was.

To my delight a mini-bus full of family and friends including the Pastor of our church, Betty Ryan, had made the journey up as well. It was a tremendous feeling to see them and we were glad they could make it. It really gave our morale a boost. Even at this late stage we had great hopes that the case would have been thrown out because of the lack of evidence, but to our disappointment things went from bad to worse.

We were offered bail set at £25,000 each in cash! Where on earth would we get that amount of money and in cash? It was impossible. The only thing that could save us was a miracle. We were told that because we could not come up with the money we would be taken to Norwich prison and appear back at Felixstowe Court the following week.

A horror of great darkness came down upon me again. We left the court and drove in the night to Norwich; it seemed to me like another 100 miles or so. I was reminded of Jesus, just before his crucifixion, being taken from Annas to Caiaphas, from Caiaphas to Pilate, from Pilate to Herod and back to Pilate again.

The "horse box" (prison bus) was freezing cold and the only people with heat were the officers driving in the front of the truck. It was also extremely uncomfortable and claustrophobic. There was a corridor down the middle of the van with five or six single cells on each side, and the four of us travelled in different compartments. I was locked into a tiny cell, about two and a half feet square. I sat, facing forward, on a wooden seat with my hands handcuffed together, but with no seat belt. I could just see out of the window at one side. I knew Len, Ralph and James were also in the vehicle but I couldn't see them, so the journey was lonely, tiresome and it seemed as if it would never end. It seemed that the driver was taking the long way round on purpose. I felt totally sick as I tried to imagine what Norwich prison would be like. I felt like crying, but the tears wouldn't flow.

Then the truck stopped at a large wooden gate, with high walls and razor wire all around it. My heart raced.

3

Inside Out

The doors swung open and the truck drove through. We were escorted to a reception area where our handcuffs were removed.

"Name?"

"Anthony Millen."

"Age?" the man's voice was bored and totally disinterested as he noted all my details on his form.

"Thirty eight."

"Right, Millen," said a younger guard "Here's a blanket and a pillow for each of you. You're in luck - there's no room in the main block for any more tonight, so you lot will go on the hospital wing. Grab this and follow me." He escorted us to the hospital wing where we were each allocated a cell and then locked up. All I could see from the window was a brick wall. The cell contained a bed, chair, cupboard and a bucket for use as a toilet. In no way did it remind me of a hospital. Alone in the cell, I sat on the bed and the now familiar feeling of loneliness and despair rose inside me. I thought of how one minute you are a free person and the next you are in prison charged for a crime you know nothing about. My mind kept going from one thought to another trying to figure it out, but coming to no conclusion at all.

It had been a long day and I crawled into bed. It was absolutely freezing that night; it was unbelievable. I slept in my clothes, I had to, and even then I kept drifting in and out of sleep because of the cold.

The next morning the cell door opened and I was taken to have a wash and a shave and empty my bucket. I found it difficult to believe that such an inhuman system still existed in modern Britain. I felt degraded and somehow ashamed. I wanted to hide myself and my bucket, even though I knew everyone else was also carrying one. On the way to the wash room I met up with my companions. After that I was returned to my cell, locked up and given breakfast. The food was lousy. Porridge, tea and boiled egg might sound quite reasonable; the problem was in the way it was cooked and the length of time it took to reach us. The porridge was lumpy and half-cooked, the egg was hard-boiled and dry and the tea was cold. I just couldn't come to terms with it no matter how hard I tried.

After breakfast I sat on the bed again considering what was happening to me. The minutes seemed to go on and on, but at least I had time to pray and reflect on the Word of God.

"Oh Lord, hear my prayer..."

"Oh God help me now..." No, it was no good, everything seemed so blank. I couldn't focus on my prayer and I couldn't pray effectively. However, I knew I had to remain strong for the sake of the others; Ralph hadn't yet fully made up his mind to serve God; Len had been a Christian, but had lost his commitment along the way, and James had only recently become a Christian. I was trying hard to stay in good shape for when Cheryl and the children came to visit. Although it was such a degrading situation to be in, I didn't want them to see me looking cast down or humiliated.

After a while I heard footsteps coming down the corridor and a woman officer pushed some envelopes and writing paper under the cell door.

"Hey! Stop a minute, lady!" I called out to her, hoping she would help me. "Tomorrow's Sunday," I explained as she put her head round the door, "and me and the other three guys that came in with me always worship God on Sundays. Where can we go in this place for prayers? We need to be with other believers to worship on a Sunday, not locked up all on our own." She looked rather surprised as she opened the door, as if this wasn't one of the usual complaints, but she agreed she would find out and let me know.

The hours passed slowly. I could make out Jim's voice from across the corridor; it sounded as though he was trying to speak about his christian faith to another inmate. Apart from that there was very little to break up the day. There were no recreational facilities. Breakfast was followed by lunch and lunch was followed by dinner. The day drew to a close and all lights were switched off.

The following morning the same monotonous routine started all over again. This time at least we had something to look forward to - a service of worship for the four of us. Just before breakfast the same officer had come to my cell and told me that we had been granted permission to worship together in a TV room near what looked like a proper hospital wing. To our delight many other inmates from the hospital wing came to join us and asked if we could pray for them. They had many different problems - Aids, mental problems, drug problems and all kinds of illnesses. We felt joy that day. Despite our own afflictions we were able to help others.

"Right lads! Time's up." We were brought back to the present by one of the two prison officers who had remained in the next room the whole time. From there they could watch what was going on; they could see our every move, but I had almost forgotten about them, as they stood impassively waiting. Now they supervised the return to our cells and told the four of us that we were going to be transferred the next day to the main prison. I felt apprehension and wondered what it would be like. I wondered whether the four of us would be allowed to share cells, or whether they would put us with other inmates.

At about 6.30 p.m. the following day we were taken to the main wing. As we walked along the corridor I lost count of the number of doors the officer unlocked for us and locked again behind us. Finally we came to the main door. When it was opened we stopped dead in our tracks. It was a shocking sight. I had never seen so many men in one place. It was worse than a cattle market. Hundreds of men chattering, different kinds of music playing, men walking up and down, keys jangling, doors banging. Poor Ralph was distraught and took a step backwards. His words were, "Jesus God Almighty above". I looked at him and saw fear across his face. I was so sorry for him.

Norwich was an old Victorian prison and it was cold and draughty. We were taken up to the next landing and allocated our cells. The escort officer said that there was a cell for two to share, but the rest of us would have to share with other inmates. Ralph jumped to accept it together with Len. That left James and myself to share with someone else. Under our breath we began praying that God would put us together in one cell. Our prayer was heard and answered when the officer asked a prisoner if he would like to share with his friend and give his cell to James and myself. He agreed. As soon as we got into the cell we began to pray. It was our great wish that on Friday, when we had to appear again before Felixstowe Magistrates Court, the court would release us and we would be allowed to go home. Together we planned a prayer and fast for our release that weekend.

During association time (when prisoners are allowed to have contact with other prisoners on the same block) we were allowed in each other's cells, where we spent the time praying and discussing what had befallen us. We tried the best way we could to cope with prison life. But it was not easy; of course it was not meant to be easy. The food was bad enough - totally dreary and unappetising; but much worse was the indescribable monotony of the place. Day after day it was the same routine. Everything was programmed to the last detail. When we ate, when we slept, when we washed and when we were allowed out of the cell, was all programmed. Added to this, it was cold. The nights especially were freezing cold. At one time I remember I could not sleep for the cold; I was already using all my available clothing and bedding, and was forced to get up and put a pair of underpants on my head in an effort to keep it warm! This reminded me of when the Apostle Paul was writing to Timothy from his prison cell and asked him to bring his cloak because he was feeling the cold.

Three days went slowly by and at last Ralph, Len, James and myself had a visit from our families and our Pastor. It was their first visit since we had been sent to Norwich. They looked well as they sat opposite us at the long "snake" table and it was some comfort for us to see them there. But at the same time it was an intensely painful experience. There was no privacy. There were officers everywhere watching every move. Our hearts sank when our families had to leave. By the look on Cheryl's face I could see how difficult she was finding it, although she tried so hard to be brave. I wished so much I could go with her. Our wives all put on a brave face - until they were out of sight - because they did not want to distress us further. But how we wished we were going home with them!

Ralph most of all was finding it very difficult to come to terms with his incarceration. He told every inmate he came across that he was innocent, and that he would be going home that weekend. When the other inmates heard the details of the case they told him that no way was he going home with such a case as that, and that made him worse.

Friday finally arrived and, with our clothes in plastic prison bags, we were taken handcuffed to a waiting coach which took us to Felixstowe. We were excited at the prospect that this was our last day in prison and that we were going home. We prayed all the way, asking God that he would change the bail requirements, so that we could meet them. After we arrived I overheard the escorting officer tell another officer not to disturb the seal on our belongings as he was sure that we were going back to Norwich that night. Under my breath I rebuked the lying spirit and continued to believe in my heart that I was going home that afternoon.

We stood before the Magistrates once again and listened as the terms of our bail were indeed changed from £25,000 cash to security. Our Pastor stood for Len and one by one our families and friends stood up to put their homes up for security on our behalf. Our families and neighbours wept as that afternoon we walked out of Felixstowe Magistrates Court. God had answered our prayers.

That Friday night all four of us headed for church and quietly walked in. It was a prayer meeting, and no doubt the brethren were praying for us when suddenly - there we were among them. Shouts of praise erupted from the congregation when they noticed us walking in. They said we reminded them of the three Hebrew boys in Daniel when they came out of the fiery furnace, (except of course that there were four of us!)

4

The Time in Between

"It's such a complete waste of time, I just can't wait to be shot of it," I complained; I was tired of going every evening to sign on at the police station, as the terms of my bail required. Cheryl had a more practical view,

"Well, the important thing is that we've got you home with us, that means everything to me and the children. For goodness sake don't risk it by forgetting to sign on again!" It was true, I had once forgotten, and had been speedily visited by a policeman threatening immediate imprisonment if it happened again. It had been a very frightening experience; the ring at the door, the uniformed police officer checking my name and asking why I hadn't signed on. When I realised in horror that I had completely forgotten, and the possible consequences, I rushed out of the door, anxious to put the matter right. The policeman had to restrain me and suggest that I should put on my shoes and my coat. It had been a genuine oversight on my part, there seemed so much to do, going backwards and forwards from solicitors' offices, reading statement after statement from Customs officers and giving statements.

"Not long now!" Ralph cheerfully reminded me, "Soon all this will be over and we can get back on with our lives again."

May 1992 was the month set for the old style committal hearing at Ipswich. We were all looking forward to it. We knew our own innocence and felt that there could be no real evidence against us. We would be glad to have it all out in the open and properly sorted out.

The four of us travelled together to Ipswich. Apparently the hearing had to be at Ipswich because it was the nearest court to Felixstowe, the port of entry of our shipment. We travelled with our wives in the church mini-bus and it only took just over an hour to get there. But once there, we had difficulty finding our way round the one-way system. We had no instructions, and finding a suitable parking space was a big problem, as we had no idea how long everything would take. Still, we had left in plenty of time and arrived in time to meet our solicitors. The four of us went into separate rooms with our solicitors while our wives waited on hard benches in the corridor outside the courtroom. The magistrates courtroom itself was a small room with one magistrate sitting at his desk, advised every so often by his clerk who sat at a separate table slightly in front of the magistrate. It was difficult to believe that such a large chunk of our lives would be decided in this small room.

Once proceedings had started, things happened fairly quickly. First Len, then James was acquitted; as we expected, they had no case to answer. Our delight was unbounded, I was already planning how to share the good news with the family.

"Name?" now it was my turn.

"Anthony Millen."

The magistrate turned the papers over on his desk, peered at some details and leaned across to speak in a low voice to the clerk. Then he cleared his throat :

"Anthony Millen, this court recommends that you stand trial for the specified charges. This court is prepared to extend the period of bail until the time of trial." I was gutted. I had been so sure that the facts would stand up for themselves, and that it would be absolutely clear that none of us had done anything illegal. To add to my misery, I became aware that the same thing was happening to Ralph.

The magistrate ruled that he also had a case to answer. We returned to London with our hopes dashed. We couldn't believe this had happened to us. I was still glad for Len and James; they had been in the depths of despair, and now they could celebrate. They were free men.

I was not free. But for some time life continued with a semblance of normality. I could still live at home with my family, (as long as I remembered the daily visit to the police station,) run the business with Ralph and continue with my preaching engagements.

17th July 1992 stands out in my memory. That was the day Customs returned our container; over half the consignment was ruined, especially the confectionery which had been stored for too long in non-ideal conditions. Of course, the whole consignment of ackees, (the 20 boxes allegedly containing drugs) which had been worth over £10,000, was missing. Our total loss was enormous, and we wondered if we would ever get the business onto an economic footing again.

17th July was also the day that the beloved pastor of our church, Sister Betty Ryan, died. It came as a big shock to me, as I had been speaking to her only hours earlier. My first thought was - who could possibly take her place as Pastor of our Edmonton church. As a deacon assisting the pastor I knew very well how essential her role had been. I wondered sadly what would happen now, and how the church was going to be run. I did not have long to wait for an answer. That evening a special meeting of the members of the congregation was called, and I was invited to be the pastor of Edmonton Shiloh Pentecostal Church.

In the midst of our bail requirements, Ralph and I continued with our business the best we could. We had started out with such enthusiasm just over a year ago. Now it was a big effort fitting it in between the daily visits to the police station, and communicating with solicitors. I lost a lot of weight at that time, and felt under a great burden; we had lost our pastor, I had new responsibilities in the church and had the impending court case to face. I was also working hard to get the business on a firm footing. Even so, it was encouraging to know that we had correctly assessed the market. Our goods were selling well and it was clear that people still wanted the products we were importing from Jamaica. The step we had taken the previous year must have been in the right direction.

5

Setting Up the Business

During this difficult time it gave me some encouragement to think back to how the business had first been set up. Ralph and I had both been made redundant in the Summer of 1991, and after various discussions and enquiries we came to the conclusion that we would form a business importing foodstuffs from Jamaica. Initially we had gone around from shop to shop making enquiries as to which were the fastest selling products on the market from Jamaica. We were told that they were Ackees (a kind of fruit), Callaloo (a type of spinach), Irish Moss (a health drink) and confectionery. We also contacted the Jamaican High Commission in London to get more information.

Our first task was to organise the company. We had to visit an office in the City where we tried to get a name of our choice. We asked for Millen and Ford, that being our two surnames, or Ford and Millen; we weren't fussy. Unfortunately that was not possible as there were companies already trading with that name. We were then told that we had to purchase a ready made company name - S.I.O Limited (Sort It Out Limited). This would definitely not have been my own choice of name, and it caused great hilarity to Cheryl when I first told her, and later provoked some dry humour in court when the prosecuting barrister commented "It seems this was not a very clever way of Sorting Things Out."

After purchasing the company, the most difficult part was trying to get the bank to assist us in securing a loan.

This proved impossible, so we started with the money we already had from our redundancy payment.

The Jamaican Embassy based in Central London advised us that in order to export anything from Jamaica we had to register with Jampro, an agency which would assist with import and export in Jamaica.

We then arranged to travel to Jamaica on a four week trip. We intended to visit different factories, checking out their prices and arrange a shipment. We arrived in Jamaica and Ralph stayed with his parents in Manchester (Jamaica). I stayed with other friends and we met up a couple of days later. Winston, an old friend of mine, took us around to various food processing factories as we did not know any. We made enquiries about shipping the products, but were told that we could not export the products under our company's name unless the company was registered in Jamaica. We wondered what we could do, as it would take a long time to get the company registered and we were only booked for four weeks. We were in a dilemma until a door of mercy was opened unto us. We were told that we could treat the matter as a one off shipment using our own name. (Praise be to God). We then contacted a shipping company who helped us to make all the necessary arrangements. We collected the goods ourselves from the factories, took them to the shippers and watched them being loaded into the container. There were Customs and Police officers there also observing the loading and sealing of the container. We could only afford to buy little more than half of a full container, but this was only the beginning. With God's help we would one day afford a full one.

While we were in Jamaica I took the opportunity to preach in various Churches at the invitation of different ministers in the area. There was a shortage of pastors and my preaching engagements escalated; as I spoke at one church I would be invited to speak at others. The churches were of all sizes; one Sunday I might be preaching to 400 people and the next to only a handful.

We returned to England and the container was delivered to us. In general we did well in selling the products and had sold almost everything within eight weeks. We were very pleased and began to consider using the profit to arrange a further shipment.

Then in September of 1991 I went alone to Jamaica. Ralph and I decided that to save money on air fares I would make the necessary arrangements in Jamaica. So I made all the purchases and had the goods delivered to the shipping company. On this occasion, I purchased three quarters of a full container load and again I watched the loading of the container together with Customs and Police Officers.

I returned home and again the products sold very quickly, especially as it was coming up to Christmas. Also we were at an advantage with many retailers as we were willing to go to their shops and deliver to them rather than waiting for them to come to us.

We now began to plan a further trip, realising that we could sell the products within 8 - 12 weeks. We began to consider whether it was necessary for us to go to Jamaica to arrange the shipment. Even after successfully completing two shipments, the bank was still unwilling to assist in providing us with a loan. But we now knew for sure that we were providing goods that people wanted, and we looked forward optimistically to expanding our business.

6

The Fateful Trip

So we began planning the third fateful trip in December 1991. Around this time my mother-in-law was also planning to visit Jamaica. Her father had died two years earlier and the custom in Jamaica was to have a remembrance celebration when the headstone was put on the grave. The family were therefore waiting for her to return for the "tombing". She wanted to travel with me and I began to make plans for the journey. At this time as well Ralph's wife, Sarah, said she was making arrangements to go to Jamaica as she had received a telegram to say her mother was very ill. Eventually we all agreed we would travel together. I booked for three weeks for Sarah and myself, and Cheryl's mother would stay for longer.

We flew to Jamaica on the 14th January 1992. I took a sum of money with me, arranging for Ralph to send the rest. We were negotiating to apply for a loan in order to do a full consignment, but it hadn't come through before I left.

When we reached Jamaica, Sarah went to stay with her mother on the North Coast. My mother-in-law and I went to her relations in the St. Elizabeth area. After a couple of days' rest I began straightaway to make arrangements for the shipment as I did not have very much time. As usual I went to Jampro, the Government Agency. I was already registered with them and I notified them that I intended to make a shipment within the next two weeks. By the end of the week I went with Winston to the Tijule factory. He had helped me before with the arrangements for the previous shipments.

We arrived, went into the office and met the owner. I gave her my estimated order of ackees, a traditional Jamaican dish packed in tins. I also ordered seasonings and bottles of sauce, and said I would ring back the following day to confirm the exact amount. She mentioned to me that she would be going away on holiday in ten days time and that I should make sure that all the paper work was done before she left. The order for the ackees was the first to be put in as this product would require a certificate from The Food and Hygiene Department in Kingston. This would take some considerable time to process. The remaining items did not require such a certificate.

The following week I went to another factory and placed an order for the drinks and confectionery. I also went to book a container and was given a date for the 1st February which I later had to cancel. During this time I was in constant contact with Ralph on the phone to sort out the exact orders we should place and he informed me that the loan had still not arrived. Ralph advised me to purchase what I could with what money I had and return without the loan. That did not make a lot of sense; I did not have enough money to purchase sufficient goods to make the trip worthwhile. So I suggested that I should wait a few more days in the hope of the money coming through, and if it still had not arrived I should leave the shipment in the hands of a friend to whom we could send the money when it was available.

Over the next few days, I was in touch with Sarah and I hired a car and went to visit her. I stayed the night with her family and together we returned to St. Elizabeth. She wanted to get to know the area as she and Ralph were hoping to return home from Britain once they had both retired from work.

It was becoming clear that as I had only booked to be in Jamaica for three weeks on this visit I would not be able to finalise all the details of the shipment. I guessed that Winston would be willing to do this, as he had helped with all previous consignments. I was also hoping that he would be able to supervise future consignments, so that I would not need to travel to Jamaica each time we needed a shipment. He willingly agreed to this, but wanted to change the arrangements for collecting the goods.

"You know how *slow* they are at that Tijule factory, Tony," he said, "if I was collecting from there on the day of shipment I'd be terrified that I'd miss the sailing time! I'd much rather pick up the ackees as soon as they're available, store them here, at my place, and then I'd be able to get them to the wharf in plenty of time." It was true, they were slow; they always acted like they'd never heard of a clock or a timetable. But still, I didn't like this new idea.

"No, that doesn't make sense," I reasoned "you're miles and miles from Tijule! It would mean paying for a truck to bring them from Tijule to here, and paying again to get them to the dock. It's a stupid idea!"

"Who are you calling stupid!" he snapped. "Look, Tony, if you're going to leave it with me, and you want me to do it, then let me handle it my way." He had a point, but I wasn't going to give in so easily.

"We've managed OK before," I said. "We've always got the goods to the wharf in time, haven't we?" Well we had; but it was always a head-ache. We had to start really early with the truck, and pick up from the various factories and food outlets in turn. A delay at any of them would make us really nervous of missing the shipment. When everything had been collected we had to drive to the shipping agents yard in time to get all the goods packed into the container, under the supervision of Customs officials. Only then could the whole lot be sent to Kingston wharf, ready for shipping. Everything had to be done very quickly, on the same day, and it had always been a great relief when it was gone.

"OK so it worked before," he retorted. "But it's getting bigger isn't it? You said you're aiming for a full size container next time. It's not going to work, Tony. Even this time we're loading over 200 cases of ackees with another 800 cases containing the drinks, confectionery and other food stuffs. You're going off and leaving me with all the donkey work. If you want me to do your shipping for you, let me get on with it. You pay for the ackees and I'll collect them. I'll get some guys to help me unload them and load them up again. I'll get everything to the wharf on time. Trust me. Look mate, if this thing takes off, I'll get a storage room built on here - specially for your precious consignments."

"OK, mate," I said wearily, "you're on; and - thanks!"

I gave in, and took the easy option.

Time was quickly passing and together with Cheryl's mother and Sarah I decided to visit relatives and do a bit of sight seeing around the Island before we left. I also took the opportunity to preach in various churches.

Sometime between the 27th and 30th January I went back to the factories and placed my final orders. Sarah said she would come with me for the drive. I had just enough to pay for the ackees, and nothing else. At this time Winston was waiting outside with some of his helpers to load the ackees onto the truck to take it back to his house. Sarah and I left to do some sight-seeing and visit my sister. When we returned Winston had already unloaded the ackees into a bedroom downstairs.

Once again I got back in touch with Ralph about the loan, but he was still having problems. I was beginning to get worried, and I had to cancel the container I had booked, and put it off until a later date. I remember at this time that the shipping company asked me if they could place a table in my container for some tourists who wanted it shipped back to London, and I agreed.

Since my return flight was booked for the 5th February, I

passed all the arrangements on to Winston. On the 3rd and 4th February I began preparations to come home, buying presents for the children and so on. My mother-in-law said at this time that she did not wish to stay any longer in Jamaica and asked me to change her flight so that she could return with Sarah and myself. I made one last telephone call to Ralph and finally he said that the money was on the way. However, it was too late for me to make the final shipping arrangements, and after talking it over with Winston I opened a joint account with him so that the money could come straight to him.

Finally, on the 5th February we all left for England. I had a most strange feeling coming back on the plane. I had a gut feeling that something was not right, but I didn't know what. A few days after arriving home, I was in touch with Winston by phone. He told me the money had duly arrived and that he had hired a truck to collect the ackees from his home. He told me he had a few guys to help him out in the loading and unloading. He told me of the expected date of arrival of the container, and that he had collected all the appropriate paperwork.

During the week before its arrival I was in touch with the incoming agents who informed me the container vessel was due to dock on the 1st March. I remember the clerk there telling me that there was a document missing which should have come from Jamaica and that the shipment could not be cleared. I quickly telephoned Winston in order for him to phone the shippers in Kingston and sort it out. I was rather surprised to be told by the home-help at his home that he was in England, but I could not believe it, and I dismissed the whole idea. It could not be. He would surely have told me, when I was in Jamaica, if he was planning a trip to England. Why would he keep it a secret. Why couldn't he tell us if he was coming? I decided that it just wasn't true. I then telephoned his place of work only to be told the same thing. I gave up and telephoned the shippers myself. They admitted that they had forgotten to send the document the agents needed and that they would send it by courier. Some days later the incoming agents confirmed that everything was in order and that the container would be delivered on the 11th March. To my surprise they asked me to send a cheque for their fees that very same day, something they didn't usually ask for. I did as they asked.

Sometime around this time, one Friday round about the beginning of March, I received a telephone call from a woman asking whether I had any ackees for sale, and wishing to come to the warehouse to pick them up. She said she was in the Brixton area, so I explained to her that I often delivered goods in that area and that I would be able to deliver to her. She phoned back again on the Saturday and I arranged to make a delivery to her shop. This meant that I had to go out of my way to buy ackees just for her and deliver them, but she was a potential new customer and so I made the effort. However, on delivery, neither the shop or the woman existed. Someone else was trading from that address. I returned home very puzzled by it all. It was the first time anyone had done anything like this to me. But why?

Later the same day Winston phoned asking whether the container had arrived. I guess there was nothing unusual about this, after all he had shipped the container and he was making sure that I had received it. I told him I had not yet received it as it was Customs and Excise practice to search it before it was delivered to me. I explained to him that I had been trying to get him by phone, but was told he was in England. He then went on to explain that he had had an argument with his wife and was in fact in a hotel in Kingston and not in England. He said he only told his home-help that he was going to England, just to get everyone off his back. I then commented to him 'how near he sounded', but he assured me he was in Jamaica, and that if I didn't believe him I should put the phone down and ring him back. There was no need to disbelieve him and so I did not phone him back. I believed him, because just before the container was delivered to me, I again telephoned Jamaica and I got him at his home.

So many times in the months following that shipment, I puzzled over the events of my last trip to Jamaica. There had been things that seemed strange at the time, and each time I reflected on it now, in the light of the drugs charge, there were other things that didn't quite tie up; questions in my mind that I could not answer. I still firmly believed that the truth would come out, and that justice would be done. If others had acted illegally, I reasoned, that would eventually come out in court. Surely that was what the judicial system was for, wasn't it? At this stage it never occurred to me that I might eventually be involved in an intricate DIY justice job in order to vindicate myself. At this time it was enough to look ahead to the hearing now fixed for 27th July 1993.

I was disappointed and very concerned when my appointed barrister pulled out of the case just two weeks before the hearing. The reason he gave was that his previous case was taking longer than he had expected. That left my new barrister with only two weeks to read up on my papers. An uneasy feeling settled on me that truth and justice might not be automatically waiting just around the corner.

7

The Trial

"From the rising of the sun
Until the going down of the same
The Lord's name is to be praised."

It was a summer's day, the sun was shining, and the church mini-bus was full of singing people. But this was no ordinary church outing, or preaching engagement. This was Tuesday, July 27th 1993. It was the first day of the trial for Ralph and me, and for me it was to prove as tragically memorable as that cold March day sixteen months earlier when we first had handcuffs thrust upon us.

Several friends travelled with us to Ipswich for the trial. We arrived early and were delighted to be met by some fellow Christians from our sister church in Ipswich. We felt quietly confident - until we met with our barristers who were not so optimistic. My previous barrister had left the case only two weeks before the hearing, so I was pleased that I had been able to get another barrister whom I knew and trusted. He was a young, black man with a Barbadian accent. But when we went into a room to speak with the barristers I was taken aback to be told that my solicitor was on holiday, and that I would be represented by a solicitor's clerk whom I did not know.

The barristers seemed to be of the opinion that the Crown would be going for conviction one way or the other. It sounded to me as if they needed some-one behind bars as quickly as possible, to demonstrate that action was being taken on drug-related crime. It seemed of less importance whether they got the right people, or whether they had sufficient evidence.

"This christianity thing of yours," my barrister said gloomily "it's probably OK in your own church in London; but I'm afraid it won't go down very well in court. Have you considered trying to shift the blame on to the man who packed the container?"

No, I certainly had not considered such a thing. I had no idea who might have been responsible for this crime, and I had no intention of blaming some-one else unless I knew the facts for sure. Still, I gained strength from knowing that God was with me, and that His promise was that He would never leave me nor forsake me. I rested on His word.

It was good to have the physical support of our families, too. At least I could see Cheryl in the courtroom, even if I wasn't allowed to speak to her. I wasn't allowed to speak to anyone, not even to Ralph when we were sitting waiting in the corridor.

We were escorted into the dock and the jury was sworn in. I thought back to the last time I had been in Ipswich, fourteen months ago, when I had been so sure that the court would see that none of us had a case to answer. Then we were in the old style committal court, now we were at the Crown Court across the road. At least on that occasion James and Len were declared to be innocent men. We could still be thankful for that. Since then Ralph and I had had a dark cloud of doubt hanging over our heads, and perhaps I was no longer as confident in the whole system of British justice as once I had been.

The court rose as the Judge took his seat. The first two days or so of the trial were mostly taken up by witnesses for the prosecution. One of these was the person I had wrongly assumed to be the "driver's mate" of the container lorry on the day I was arrested. I now knew that he had been a plain clothes Customs officer. At last I understood why the gates of the warehouse were already unlocked when we got there, and why this man had been so concerned that we didn't touch a wire on the container - it was a bugging device. In court it was stated that they had a record of everything we had said to each other while we were unloading the container. But it was not produced in court.

On the first day we noticed a blue folder on the Judge's table. I was later told that this was a *voir dire*. It was an application by the crown to read into evidence a statement from their "absent" witness in Jamaica. This was the man who had packed my container, who they now said was afraid to come to England.

"Afraid of who, or what?" I asked, but the question was never answered. The *voir dire* was fiercely opposed by our legal team, but to no avail. The Judge ruled that it could be read out. He stated that there was no unfairness to either Ralph or myself to read it out. I did not understand how he could have said that, knowing that it is impossible to cross-question a written statement. Without it the crown would have had a hard time proving their case.

After this ruling the Judge declared a recess and left the court. My barrister, who had been looking decidedly displeased with the decision to allow the *voir dire,* snatched off his wig in disgust and threw it onto the floor. He then picked it up and marched out of the room. Unfortunately I did not have long to consider the matter, as the time had come for Ralph and me to be put into the witness box.

I was first to be questioned. I declined to swear on the Bible and accepted the alternative of making a solemn affirmation. This surprised some people who knew I was a Christian, but I believe that what the Bible says is true; I try, with God's help, to live my life according to what the Bible says, so it does not make sense to disregard the words of Jesus,

"Do not swear at all.....Simply let your 'yes' be 'yes' and your 'no' be 'no'."

"Can you give the court, please, your name and address and how old you are, Mr. Millen," asked my barrister. Then I was examined by Ralph's barrister.

The days dragged on. From July 27th to August 10th I drove the mini-bus every day from Edmonton to Ipswich with our loyal supporters. It was tiring, of course, but at least I could go home at night, which was a relief. There had originally been some talk of being locked up for the duration of this trial. Cheryl and the other wives attended court every day in spite of the journey and their anxiety about the whole affair. My children had come with us on the first day, but they were not allowed into the court, so we made arrangements to leave them at home after that.

Each day after the morning break we would go back to our Ipswich church for lunch and a session of prayer. The Lord bless our Ipswich brothers and sisters; they were a tower of strength to us.

When it was my turn to be examined by the prosecuting barrister I was confused and upset by his methods. I was totally taken aback by the way the court conducted itself. It did not seem simply to be trying to get at the truth. If only I had known how the legal machine worked! In retrospect, I wish I had seen a court case before. I didn't realise that the prosecution's job was to get a conviction.

"Mr. Millen, somebody went to a lot of trouble to hide the drugs in these tins didn't they?"

"I don't know," I replied.

"It has been described as a sophisticated concealment wouldn't you agree?"

"I don't think so, the boxes were lighter than usual," I said.

"You're not telling us the truth, are you Mr. Millen? I noticed that when you came into the witness box you didn't want to take the oath on the Bible did you?"

"No," I replied.

"But you have just told us that after the delivery, you

were thanking God for the delivery of the ackees weren't you? Do you normally say your prayers when a container of ackees and callaloo and so on is delivered?"

"I always pray without ceasing," I replied.

"Call yourself a Christian, Mr Millen! You're nothing but a hypocrite." This man had not understood at all that the reason for me not swearing on the Bible was because of my christian faith. He also seemed to have difficulty in understanding that normal people might pray and praise God about ordinary everyday events. This really seemed to enrage him, and he seemed to me to be muddying the waters, saying things that were irrelevant to the case. He asked me what I knew about the 'Yardies' - a notorious Jamaican drugs gang. I told him I knew nothing about them except what I read and saw on the television. The Crown seemed to be suggesting that our company was a sham, and that its real object was to import cannabis. But when they could not find a way to say just how I could have got the money to pay for £750,000 of drugs, they resorted to the bizarre suggestion that the drugs were obtained on credit!

That weekend we returned home to London, but I spent most of the week-end lost in thought. In my mind I was going over and over the court case. I received many phone calls from my friends and relatives. They all tried to comfort me and assure me that God was on our side. If God was for us, they reasoned, then who could be against us? He would never allow us to go to prison. So many friends tried to re-assure me in this way, that it was easy to believe what they were saying.

On Monday we returned to Ipswich. There were always at least fifteen people in the mini-bus, including Cheryl, who went every day. Friends from the Ipswich church also attended, so the court was always full. On the last day our three daughters, Marilyn, Shantel and Leonie also attended.

The case dragged on for 15 weary days until at last the prosecution rested their case. Then the Judge became an extended arm of the prosecution and proceeded to ask me about my financial dealings in Jamaica. I told him all there was to tell, but still not satisfied he told me he could have everything checked out. Now it was time for the Judge to give his summing up. I had given evidence for two days yet he summed up in less than 10 minutes. His Honour seemed very dismissive and disparaging in his remarks about me in particular, and selected to remind the jury of what he thought was important to him. I thought he made it clear to all that he was of the opinion that I was not telling the truth, and he seemed to intimate as much to the jury.

The jury retired at 12.08 p.m. We spent the time waiting in prayer. They were brought back at 4.33 p.m., but they had not reached a verdict. The Judge then urged them to go back and try to reach a verdict. News came at 5.44 p.m. that they had reached a verdict. This was it - one way or another our fate was to be sealed by a group of ordinary men and women who could not possibly know all the facts.

"Members of the jury, have you reached a verdict in respect of each defendant?"

"Yes."

"How do you find the defendant Anthony Millen, guilty or not guilty?"

"Guilty."

"How do you find the defendant Ralph Ford, guilty or not guilty?"

"Not guilty." The blood drained from my body and I didn't know how I managed to stay on my feet. I was being sent to prison for a crime I did not do.

"What inspired you to embark on this venture I do not know," said his Honour. "It was the height of folly, having regard to your life in the community and the commitments to your family. The minimum sentence I can impose and the minimum sentence I do impose, is to send you to prison for eight years. Take him down."

8

From Pulpit to Prison

Tuesday 10th August 1993 was the worst day of my life. My dream of freedom was once and for all shattered. Everything was wiped out by a single word of "Guilty". I even told the Judge that he was making a mistake, and that I was not guilty. I was totally stunned; I could not get my mind round it. I could not understand how this man could be a judge and yet he couldn't even judge whether a man was innocent or guilty. How many other innocent people had he sent to prison? But it seemed that nobody cared how many lives had been ripped apart, as long as somebody paid the price. They called this a justice system. Now I was going to be torn away from my wife and family. My only son, Jonathan, was just seven years old, how was he going to cope without me? I was numb with shock, I wanted to cry, but I couldn't. It didn't seem real to me; it was like something you read in a novel, or watched on t.v.

I was led away, taken down some stairs and put in a cell. They were the steepest stairs I had ever seen. If the shock of the sentence didn't make you collapse then the stairs certainly would. This was it: now I was a convicted drug smuggler as far as the system was concerned. My life was in ruins. My barrister brought me little comfort when he came to see me.

"Of course we'll appeal, Mr Millen. Now you really must not worry so much about this little set back. Eight years doesn't mean eight years, you know. At the most you'll probably only have to do four."

"I'm innocent! I shouldn't have to do any," I cried, and I imagined that it would only be a matter of a few months and I would be out.

But what was going to happen to me now? The thoughts kept whirling through my head. Why? why? why? I hadn't done anything to deserve this. I was in a daze. My wife and my daughters came down to see me. The eldest, Marilyn, was 16; Shantel was 12 and Leonie was ten. We had left Jonathan in London as he was not old enough to go into the court. This brought me back to reality. They were crying and as I looked at them I was heartbroken. They didn't say anything much, they were in a state of shock just as I was. All I could say was "Don't worry. Do your best to manage." After a few minutes they were told to go, and I bid them good-bye.

I was told to empty my pockets and was handcuffed to the other prisoners, who had had to wait until a verdict was reached in my case. They swore at me and blamed me for them having to miss 'tea time' back at the prison. I was led outside to the waiting coach bound for Norwich prison. The coach drove past the court and as I looked out I saw my family and brethren sitting on the wall weeping. It reminded me of Jesus as they led Him away. There were those who bewailed and lamented Him and He told them:

"Weep not for me, but weep for yourselves and your children."

I tried to hum a song to myself to try to lift my spirit which by now was utterly cast down.

"Yes, Jesus loves me, yes Jesus loves me....." From the corner of my eye I could see the other prisoners looking at me.

"You're a madman! You've just been given eight years, and you're singing 'Yes Jesus loves me.' " They laughed me to scorn, but they didn't understand that God doesn't play games with the lives of His children. I believed that God knew what was happening to me, and that He wasn't making a mistake with my life. Satan couldn't touch me unless he had divine permission. I could not at that time see any purpose, or even any sense, in what seemed to me an unjust judgement on an innocent man. But I could accept that God would have a purpose, and that at some time in the future I might become aware of what it was.

I was lost in a world of thoughts as we reached Norwich prison that night. I felt sick as I wondered what lay in store for me. I remembered the routine as I waited my turn to be processed. I was given my clothes and bedding which consisted of a sheet, blanket, pillow case, and plastic cutlery. I was taken to the main prison and as the door opened I was met with the familiar sound of inmates milling around and shouting to each other. Norwich was a dispersal prison, so long-stay and short-stay prisoners were mixed together. I was allocated a cell - as a matter of fact almost next door to the cell I had had the week I spent in Norwich sixteen months before. I was given some cold left over pie which wouldn't go past my throat. I shoved it to one side, drank some tea and went to bed.

I spent a sleepless night going over and over and reliving the trial. It was all so unjust. I thought of the Prophet Habakkuk when he said,

"the law is slack and judgement doth never go forth: for the wicked doth compass about the righteous; therefore wrong judgement proceedeth."

How could they find me guilty? Why would I want to conceal drugs in tins when I knew that Customs went through the container with a fine tooth comb? I was a man of God and I preached against things like this. I thought about who could have put the drugs there and why. Was it another company who was trying to wipe me out? Was it the factory who tinned the ackees - were they involved in wrong dealings? Was it them, and by mistake they had put the drugs in my container? There was no way I would find out now. Then I remembered another business man to whom the same thing had happened. Drug smugglers had put drugs in his container and tracked it all the way from Jamaica; then seven of them turned up at his warehouse to collect the drugs. It was only by the grace of God that his barrister was able to prove that he did not know those seven men. I thought about my case and wondered whether the same thing had been done to my container. I never thought for a minute that anyone involved with packing the container had done this to me. People knew what kind of person I was. I dismissed the thought completely and consoled myself that with the appeal coming up soon, I wouldn't be here for long.

What an understatement this was to be! But at least it gave me something to look forward to, as I was of the opinion that appeals only took a matter of weeks! I was going to continue to protest my innocence and fight to clear my name.

9

My Name and My Roots

Millen. It's a good name, and I'm proud of it; and at 38 I didn't want it clouded with unjust accusations of illegal dealings.

I was born in Jamaica, in a parish called Clarendon. My father came to England when I was quite young - soon after I started school. In the 1950s the British government advertised extensively abroad, and particularly in the West Indies, for workers to come and assist the sadly depleted work-force. So many men had been killed in the war, that there was a serious problem in keeping basic services running. Hospitals, industry, and transport all desperately needed workers from abroad. The advertisements were very persuasive; they promised jobs and a good income; with homes and education for the workers' families. Many, many workers went to England from Jamaica; often one or both parents went first, intending to see how things worked out before sending for their families. This was the case with so many families that we knew, that it seemed absolutely normal to me.

I had two older sisters and one older brother. My mother had also gone away to find a job, leaving me and my two sisters in the care of my grandparents, on my mother's side. My mother was living and working in Kingston, the principal city of Jamaica, but she came down to "the country" to see us as often as she could, to make sure we were all getting on OK. My Gran found herself looking after other people's children, as well. These were children whose parents could not afford to look after them. Some of their parents were abroad. She didn't necessarily adopt them, but she brought them up, and their parents were quite happy with the arrangement. Gran treated us all the same. Whatever was bought for her own grandchildren was also bought for the others.

My grandfather was a farmer with at least forty acres of land, and I remember him having many employees on his farm. He was not short of money, either. During the 1950s, when things were hard for most people, he was still able to foot the bill to send seven of his children abroad so that they could better themselves. He was a member of the local Methodist church, which he attended regularly; but now, looking back, I wonder if he was a committed Christian. His life-style didn't always seem to match up to christian standards. He seemed to me to be a worldly-wise Methodist.

I started school at the age of five in "first class". In those days Junior school consisted of first, second, third class up to about 6th class.

My grandmother could not read or write, and she didn't really know what we were doing in school, or how we were getting on in our subjects. So the burden fell on my older sisters, Madje and Bev, to sort out which schools we would all go to. They kept changing from school to school, and when they changed schools I had to change too. This severely disrupted my lessons and I couldn't settle down. I began to skip school quite regularly. I would get up, get dressed and go to school in the morning, and then bunk off and head for the nearby river, where I would spend the afternoon with my friends. The more I "bunked" school, the more I began to hate lessons. The teachers seemed so cruel; we were beaten for the slightest thing. At this time my grandmother and my sisters didn't have a clue that I wasn't attending school regularly.

I went to Sunday school regularly, because my

grandmother saw to it that we went. But I found it very boring, and saw no real meaning in it, and I used to skip Sunday school as well when I could get away with it, and then go home when I knew it was over.

When I was about 12 or 13, I made up my mind that I had had enough of school and I decided to go and live with my elder brother, Patrick, in the City of Kingston. He tried to get me to learn a trade, young as I was, so I became an apprentice to an electrician. Patrick also bought me a bicycle, and in my spare time I began to deliver small parcels for local shops in the area. I was maturing quite quickly, and I began to spend more and more time with older people, rather than with friends of my own age.

My parents had by now both moved to England, where they were living and working in Leeds. My father worked in a factory and my mother was a part-time hospital auxiliary. Things were going reasonably well for them and eventually, my parents were in a position to bring me to Britain. So in March 1970, when I was sixteen years old, I also came to live in Leeds.

By this time I had two younger brothers, Durrant and Dixon, who were already living with my parents. It was a strange and difficult situation for a teen-age boy. I hardly knew my parents. In Jamaica I had grown up as the youngest in the family, and now here I was trying to fit in with a family of younger siblings. It was my family, I knew that, but sometimes it didn't feel like it and I had problems knowing what they expected of me. I found it difficult to please my parents. For a start they were horrified to learn that I had not been attending school, and I was sent on a Youth Training Scheme; I had to attend college at nights for further education. This came hard, after being out of education for several years - after all, I had been earning my living in Kingston!

And then there was their high standard of behaviour!

My parents had strict rules and regulations which came as an enormous shock to me, as I had pretty well pleased myself in Jamaica. They wanted me to dress smartly, be home at a certain time, work hard at my studies and have respectable-looking friends.

I just couldn't settle down; and I didn't like Leeds. So I decided to visit my aunt who lived in London. The pace of life in London was much faster and much more to my liking. I made up my mind that I was not going back to Leeds, and I stayed with my aunt. She had rules too, Jamaica fashion, but she was very kind to me. However, I'd only been with her for a short while when I decided to join the army. I thought that this would be a good way to learn a trade, but it didn't work out. I didn't like army life and after a short while I left. I subsequently found a job with Thorn EMI as a machine operator and worked there for a number of years.

I used to visit my parents in Leeds quite frequently and it was whilst visiting them that I met Cheryl. I remember it so clearly. It was April 1974.

When I look back now it seems we were destined to meet. I remember that the first time I saw Cheryl was in a street in Leeds. She was with her friend Valerie, and I was with two of my friends. We were all out that night looking for a party to go to. In those days we young people spent a lot of time searching for the best dance to go to. My friend Bobby recognised the girls; I had never seen them before,

"Hey Cheryl!" he called across "Where's the best party?"

"No idea, Bobby. But you could try the one in that house down there," pointing down the road.

"Thanks, love. But I guess we'll carry on sussing things out for ourselves."

My friends and I moved on, not expecting to meet up with them again. We found a party and, to my surprise, some hours later in walked Cheryl and her friend. I knew it was love at first sight. I could not take my eyes off her for the whole night. I plucked up courage and went over to ask her for a dance. We danced until the early hours of the morning and then I walked her home. I asked if she would meet me the following day and she agreed. Next day I made sure I was at the meeting point early. I couldn't stop thinking about her. I was glad when she turned up, and we went to my mother's house where we talked for a long time. We had so much in common; like me, she had grown up in Jamaica, but she had come to England when she was nine years old. Like me, she hardly knew her parents at that time, and was only now getting to know them properly. We talked and talked, delighting in each other's company. But I did not tell her then that I had recently broken up with my girlfriend; or that we had a baby of three months, called Karen.

I knew, even then, that Cheryl was some-one really special, and that I did not want to have any secrets from her. But I so much wanted our friendship to grow and develop, that I didn't want to say anything to spoil it. It was weeks before I summoned the courage to tell her about baby Karen. For various reasons we did not manage to see much of Karen during her early childhood, but now that she is grown up and living not far from us, in London, we see her often and enjoy a pleasant relationship.

In those early days Cheryl and I began writing to each other, and whenever I had a spare week-end I would go up to Leeds to see her. After a year or so Cheryl moved to London and into my rented room. After a few months we eventually found a one bedroomed flat. She soon got a job as a shorthand typist in a solicitor's office while I was still working at Thorn EMI. A year later, on March 4th 1976 our first child, Marilyn, was born. With only one wage coming in things got very difficult and we had little spare cash. We struggled on with the help of the Almighty (although at that time we did not know Him). There were times when we only had sardines and potatoes for dinner. After a while we moved into Edmonton, and on a glorious day in September 1977 we were married. Soon Cheryl found another job and for a while things became financially secure. In 1979 we moved back to Tottenham and eventually bought our own house; this is where we were living when Shantel, Leonie and Jonathan were born.

For some time I had been longing to return to Jamaica and was glad when a friend who was planning to move there suggested that we should go into business together on the Island. I decided to give it a try, and left for Jamaica. The plan was that I would get things ready for Cheryl and the family to come and join me. I looked out a suitable school for Marilyn and even went to see the teachers. I felt very optimistic about the business venture, which involved driving a mini-bus, a job which would have suited me. But my business partner pulled out; I could not handle it on my own, and so I returned to England, and got a job with Transcare Distributions.

It was around this time, sometime in 1982, that Cheryl started to attend church with a friend. One Sunday afternoon she came in from church and told me that she had "been saved". I remember that I laughed her to scorn, and she became upset. I didn't even believe in a God, and so I thought it must all be a sham. But after a while I began to notice Cheryl changing in many ways. She no longer wanted to go to clubs with me, and was quite happy to stay indoors. She also began to try her best to persuade me to go to church, but I wasn't having it. She even used to bring in her friend to try to talk to me, but I told her that I would not believe in God until I saw Him stand in front of me. I thought that would be the only thing that would convince me, at a time when I really didn't know what I was looking for.

The longing to return home did not leave me, and

another opportunity to go into business with a different friend arose. This time I was planning to go into farming, like my grandfather and his family before him. After giving the matter much thought, I accepted my friend's offer and Cheryl and I decided that I would go to Jamaica and prepare the way for my family. This was January 1984. At this time, because of Cheryl's influence, I was becoming a little more interested in God. Although many times when she was encouraging me to accept the Lord my mind was on other things - like the bets I had put on the horses and dogs, for instance.

One night, shortly before my departure for Jamaica, we were in our bedroom when Cheryl asked me bluntly if I wanted to accept the Lord as my Saviour. To my own surprise I said yes. I felt I needed help of some sort; I felt that my way of life was not enough, I wanted something more. Cheryl's life was clearly better than mine, and I wanted a bit of it! I was not too clear about the details, but at this stage I thought it was worth trying. Cheryl prayed for me and told me that not everyone got saved like the Apostle Paul on the road to Damascus, so I should not expect the thunder to roll and the lightning to flash!

I prayed the sinner's prayer with her:

"Lord, I know I am a sinner;
  I know you died on the cross for my sins;
  Forgive me for my sins.
  Wash me.
  Cleanse me in your blood,
  And make me your child."

and I left it like that. I couldn't believe that it was that easy to accept the Lord. I thought there must be more to it than that. Before I left for Jamaica some two weeks later, Cheryl bought me a Bible and gave me a *Daily Bread* booklet to read.

While I was busy with all the travelling, and trying my best to sort things out, I didn't think too much about christian matters. But I had put my hand into the hand of God, and he certainly caught up with me! Soon after I arrived in Jamaica, relationships with my business partner became sour, and we parted company. When I returned to England 16 months later, I had turned my back on my old way of life and was a committed Christian.

The dream of a new life, farming in Jamaica, had not materialised and I got a job again with Transcare Distribution, the company I had previously worked for. We settled down as a family of five, until Jonathan's arrival in 1986 made us six.

My christian faith was now very important to me, and I started preaching in my spare time. I preached in the local markets and even, occasionally, at Hyde Park Corner. I felt the hand of God upon me, and I enrolled for a three year Bible course in London, organised by the Central Bible Institute, Birmingham. The studying involved in the course was something totally new for me, and I found it very hard work. Sometimes it seemed too much and I thought of giving it up. But Cheryl was always supportive; she was a tower of strength, I don't suppose I could have carried on without her. I was also encouraged to persist by our pastor at Dalston Shiloh church, Pastor Betty Ryan. This was the same church that Cheryl had first attended with her friend. I joined later after my conversion and was soon taking an active part in the life of the church when I became a deacon and a member of the church board.

My responsibilities in the church increased enormously after I was asked to be pastor of Edmonton Shiloh Church in July 1992, following the death of Betty Ryan. I had managed to fulfil this position while I had been at home on bail, but it was a great concern to me as to what would happen now. This, then, was the life I had been snatched away from; a busy life full of family, preaching, and church involvement. More recently, there was the added excitement of the new business with Ralph. This time it looked as though we were going to be successful; we had done our home-work carefully and it seemed we had identified a real need in the market. It was obviously going to involve a lot of hard work, but we were ready for that.

This was my life, the life I wanted to get back to, as quickly as possible. But would it be as easy as I hoped?

10

Faith on Trial

When morning arrived on 11th August 1993, I was still in a state of severe shock. I could still hear the Judge saying,
"I am sending you to prison for eight years."
I pinched myself to see whether I was dreaming, and my stomach turned over and over. I was now a convicted drug smuggler as far as society and the whole legal system was concerned. I was still unable to take it all in. I was in a daze.
I looked around the cell in Norwich Prison and saw that nothing much had changed since last year, when I had been locked up for a week with Ralph and the guys. The only improvement was that they were putting in new toilets.
At 8 o'clock the doors were opened and an officer shouted "Breakfast!"
I emerged from my cell on the top floor and stared blankly around. I observed the prisoners as they walked along on their various landings, carrying their slopping-out buckets and toiletries as they headed for the bathroom. Those buckets had served them all night and the smell was indescribable. I noticed too the wire mesh stretching across each landing. I supposed it was there to save the life of those who might feel like committing suicide, and looking at some of the inmates' faces I could understand why. Some of the men looked weary and haggard, others looked grim and menacing. As for me, I felt totally alone and so confused. I knew nobody here; I didn't understand the system and I had no idea what was going to happen to me. I wished I could have turned back the hands of time and stayed in Jamaica

and packed the container myself.

Each landing had to take their turn to collect their breakfast which was porridge, a boiled egg (if you were lucky), a bread roll and a cup of tea. I was served by another inmate and headed back to my cell to eat my breakfast. The door was slammed shut by an officer and opened again an hour and a half later. The tray was collected and the door locked again. There I had to stay until they let me out.

Not long after, an officer opened the door and escorted me downstairs to the main security office to discuss my long term allocation. A social worker and various ranking prison officers were there. They were polite, but distant. I had the feeling they didn't really regard me as a person. I was more a "case" that needed to be sorted out. During the discussion it was decided that ideally they would like to send me to the Isle of Wight or the Isle of Sheppey to serve my sentence. I had no idea where either of these places were. They sounded so foreign, and this brought some fear to my mind. It all sounded as if they were sending me to an island in no man's land. But why did they want to send me so far away from my family? I wondered. Norwich was far enough. I guess they couldn't care less. I was just a convict in the system.

"Do you think you'll be able to cope with your sentence, Millen?" asked one of the officers.

"Don't worry, I won't be here that long," I replied, still convinced that an appeal would bring my early release. For I had no idea how long appeals took to come through.

"You seem rather optimistic," he said sourly. "What about your wife, and, let me see, four children, isn't it? Are you expecting to keep in touch?"

"My wife will visit as soon as she receives the official permission," I replied quickly. "I'm sure she'll make arrangements to bring the children too. I expect she'll get help, if she needs it, from our friends and family."

In fact families could only visit when they were allowed

to, and they had to have an official visiting order from the prison. If a friend or other relative wanted to visit, a special request had to be made, and possibly visiting time taken from the family. But Cheryl visited me every single week, the whole time I was in prison. She had to drive to places she had never previously gone to; but she never missed, bless her, whatever the weather or the road conditions were like. I lived for those visits. When the weather was bad I felt torn apart, because I didn't really want her driving in fog or snow, but at the same time I desperately wanted her to come. Sometimes she brought one or more of the children with her, even when it meant keeping them out of school.

When I was returned to my cell and locked up, I sat on the bottom bunk and again started to relive the whole of my arrest and trial. The full horror of my situation was beginning to sink in. Slowly I was beginning to get bitter against all those who had contributed to my shameful incarceration and to my family being torn away from me. The more I thought about it, the more I wanted to hit back at whoever had put the drugs in those tins; and I felt hatred towards the Customs Officers, the prosecution barrister, the Judge and the jury. I felt I wanted to retaliate and somehow hurt them, for the situation I was now in. I could think only of the injustice of it all. I felt that Customs knew, really, that I wasn't guilty. It seemed to me that the Judge hadn't been just, and I bitterly resented the way he hadn't seemed to care, the impatient way he had tapped his pencil on his desk to get things moving; and I didn't like the way the jury had looked at me, in disgust and scorn, as if they were judging me on my appearance.

The day passed very slowly, and the more I prayed to God the more it seemed as if heaven had closed its doors and the ground under my knees had become like brass. It seemed as if God was nowhere to be found. It reminded me of the story of Job in the Bible, and how he felt when he said,

"If only I knew where to find him; if only I could go to his dwelling! I would state my case before him and fill my mouth with arguments. I would find out what he would answer me and consider what he would say. But if I go to the east, he is not there; if I go to the west, I do not find him. When he is at work in the north, I do not see him; when he turns to the south, I catch no glimpse of him. But he knows the way that I take; when he has tested me, I shall come forth as gold"

These words expressing the experience of some-one thousands of years ago also brought comfort to me.

A week or so into my sentence I was told I could attend a part-time education course of my choice. The choices were very limited - English, craft-making or computer studies. I chose the latter, not because I was interested in computers, but because being locked up for most of the day just added to my distress. As I had been given such a long sentence I had been placed on my own, although it seemed that many of the other inmates were two or three to a cell. When I thought further about it I wondered if it was at all possible to study in a place such as this. It certainly wouldn't be easy with so much on my mind. Sometimes when I arrived for a lesson the computer room was full so there was no opportunity to work on the computers. Instead I had to use another room where other guys were busy making rag dolls! At other times it might just be a general discussion about nothing in particular. At that time phoning my wife twice a day was the only comfort I had to break the monotony of prison life.

Phoning was possible - but not easy. There were only two phones for over 300 men, so there were always queues at the phones. Inmates would sometimes fight for their place in the queue. Then, if the person they so much wanted to speak to was not at home, they missed their turn, so that by the time they finally got through, calls might well start with recriminations, "Where were you? I told you I'd phone as soon after six as I could." Such minor inconveniences did nothing to help relationships that were already under intolerable strain. Families could not increase the call time by sending in phone cards, as only the special phone-cards which were sold in the prison could be used.

The following week Cheryl and the children came to see me. Everyone tried to put on a brave face, but inside we were all feeling empty and numb. After they had gone I went back to my cell, heartbroken. I felt so desperately alone and once more a fog of confusion covered my mind. Why had this tragedy befallen us? Couldn't God have stopped it?

"Everything works together for good"
kept coming to my mind, but what good purpose could the Lord possibly have in my situation? I slumped onto the bunk and cried to God. With tears streaming down my face I heard a still, small voice. It was the voice of the Spirit of God asking,

"Have you learnt to forgive, my son?" I dried my tears and listened again for the voice. But it never came. I knew however that it was unmistakably the voice of God. He had heard me and now his presence filled my cell. Straightaway I realised how easy it was to forgive from the lips, but not from the heart. I cried out to God once more and asked him to forgive me for my bitter feelings, and to forgive those who had put me in prison. Then and only then, the peace that passes all understanding, that I so desperately needed, came to me.

From then on I began to have a different outlook towards the system. I put to one side the bitterness and resentment and was enabled to look at the inmates the way God looked at them, and I saw that many of them were lost and in a hopeless condition both physically and spiritually. They needed to be changed - they needed a Saviour.

This was my turning point, and once I had realised the

need, I set to work giving out gospel tracts. I felt that giving out literature was the best way to reach these men. I couldn't speak to all of them and anyway, they didn't want to listen; they didn't want to waste association time talking to me about God, but they were quite happy to be given something that they could take back to their cells and read during the long, empty hours. Cheryl brought the literature in for me; she had to get them inspected by a prison officer, but she understood the importance of having something positive to hand out. Some of the men accepted them, others laughed me to scorn, but that didn't matter.

One time a group of six men surrounded me and tried to ridicule me. I felt intimidated, but was given strength to answer their faithless questions. Gradually they got tired of the sport, and one by one they wandered off until only the leader was left. But by then the anger had left him, and he had nothing more to say. He had his flask in his hand, and he carried on getting his hot water before everyone was 'banged up' (locked in their cells) for the night. Everybody had a flask for hot water. I never saw so many flasks in all my life.

In the first week of my sentence, a prison officer would look in every half hour or so. They did this to all new, long-term inmates, to make sure they were not trying to harm themselves. Sometimes they would just peer through the observation window, sometimes they would put their head round the door and say something like "Everything all right here?" or "You OK, Millen?" a meaningless comment which required no answer. On one occasion I was singing, and praying aloud in my cell. The officer on duty that night passed by at about 10.00 p.m. heard a voice in what was supposed to be a single cell and called out,

"Everything OK in there?"

"Yes thanks," I replied, "We're fine!" Quick as a flash he was into the cell,

"**We're** fine? Who've you got in there?"

"Just me and the Lord!" I answered, sweetly.

I can still remember the smell at Norwich. It was like the smell of penned animals. The antiquated cells were always frowzy, so when all the cell doors were open, at meal-times and association, there was a stale smell of men's bodies, many of them unwashed because some of the inmates had long since given up all pride in themselves. My cell was two doors from the toilet, and was never really free from the smell.

Facilities for association time were very limited, as far as I could see. There were no recreational facilities and inmates spent most of the time just going to and from each other's cell. The noise was almost overwhelming as there was a lot of shouting and swearing. I was often alone, as not many of them wanted to hear the good news of Christ. I really had nothing else to discuss and for this reason most of the inmates kept away from me. It wasn't that I didn't want to share other subjects with them, but somehow I found that there was a real barrier. I would have liked to make friends, of course. I would have liked to have been able to spend time chatting with other men with similar interests. But on the whole, the conversation of my fellow prisoners was totally different from anything I had been used to. I felt I was already alienated by my different life-style, conversation and speech. However much I wanted to make friends, they would back off almost as soon as I opened my mouth.

On one association evening I was standing alone outside my cell, leaning against the rails, watching the milling around of the other inmates and as I looked around, I noticed one young man sitting on the floor in a corner with his head between his knees. I walked over to him,

"What's up mate? Anything I can do?"

"I've tried it before," he gasped "and they stopped me.

This time I *will* do it and nobody will stop me."

"What on earth are you on about?" I asked. Then he came out with everything. It appeared that there was an organised drug business going on and he had mounted up a large debt. He couldn't pay, and the others in the drugs ring had told him to kill himself so that they didn't have to do it for him. To make matters worse, his wife had left him and he was no longer getting any visits from her or the children. This just added to his depression. He was at his wits end, and intended to commit suicide. He smelt, and was badly in need of a shower, a change of clothes and a good hair cut.

"OK mate," I said, taking a deep breath, "I reckon we can sort this out, if we take one thing at a time. Come to my cell and let's start at the beginning."

I took him to my pad, sat him down and told him that Jesus loved him and that it was wrong to take his life. Christ would help him through his crisis. He was glad for the encouragement, and after I prayed with him he accepted Christ in his life. He agreed to say the "sinner's prayer" as simply and easily as I had, all those years ago, in my bedroom with Cheryl.

"The next thing, man," I said encouragingly, "is to clean yourself up a bit. You'll feel much better when you've had a shower and got into some clean things." He was past helping himself on that one, so I gave him some soap, and some of my clean clothes, and sent him off for a shower. When he came back he was already looking slightly better.

"Now for the best bit," I said, handing him a phone card, "If I were you, I'd go and phone your wife. Tell her everything that's happened. Tell her how bad things had got; tell her you're a reformed character and you want to make a new start. Tell her how much you miss her and the kids. Then ask if she can send the money to clear your debt." Amazingly, she did; and from that day he really tried to help himself. Eventually I left him in the capable hands of one of the Chaplains, who contacted me some time later when I was transferred to Oxfordshire, to say that the man was doing well and that relationships with his family had been restored. I was ecstatic to hear how the hand of God had so wonderfully improved the life of a man who had been on the point of killing himself.

On another association evening I was outside my cell again, looking over the rails, when I noticed five men standing in a group, but one of them was behaving rather strangely - hitting the wall and the window, which was made of toughened glass, with his fists. As I looked on, the other four walked away and left him but I sensed that something was wrong, and I ran down to the next landing to see what was happening. His face was blue and covered in sweat. He was gasping for breath and desperately pounding with his fist, and it looked as if the life was leaving his body.

"Are you OK?" was the only thing I could think of saying, but obviously he couldn't respond. I came to the conclusion that he was having an asthma attack, although I had never seen one before. I put my hands on him and did what I knew to do best - I prayed. God's word says that in his name those who believe in him shall cast out devils and bring health to the sick and dying. Immediately he came round and walked off to his cell looking back at me in terrified amazement as he went. He really didn't know how close he had come to death's door and what God had done for him. Years later, when I met him in a different prison, he recognised me at once, ran out of the dinner queue to give me a bear hug, and told me that he'd never since had another attack.

The following week my personnel officer came and gave me some feedback on my sentence. He confided to me that he saw no reason for such a long sentence and said he would do all he could to send me to a brand new prison with all the facilities for long term prisoners, and nearer to my family. I would be glad to leave Norwich; it was still intensely cold inside, although it was supposed to be summer.

In September 1993 I was informed that I was being transferred to a new prison in Oxfordshire. That night I laid on my bed and wondered what lay in store for me. I also wondered why it was taking so long to hear about my appeal. I had filled in all the papers against conviction and sentence, but I hadn't heard a word.

A week later the day of my departure arrived. I packed my things and said my good-byes. I was handcuffed and escorted to the waiting prison bus. About ten other inmates were being transferred to HMP Bullingdon, in Oxfordshire, and other prisons. I remember one young man in particular, who had been convicted of baby-battering. That is one of the offences that convicts will not tolerate, and he had been beaten up in his cell. Now he was being transferred for his own safety. I wondered briefly if there was any sort of future at all he could look forward to in prison.

But my thoughts were mainly occupied with my own future. I was glad that I was being moved closer to Cheryl and the family, and I hoped this new prison would be a bit more comfortable than Norwich. Surely they wouldn't build a new prison with victorian facilities? I hoped there would be some kind of heating facility, and improved educational and leisure activities. But there was absolutely nothing I could do about it, so I would just have to wait and see. It was an uneventful journey, and by late evening we arrived at Bullingdon.

11

Through the Fire
Bullingdon

When we finally arrived at Bullingdon prison, near Bicester in Oxfordshire, we were hungry, thirsty and tired after travelling all day, dropping prisoners off at various other prisons. But as convicted criminals, there was to be no comfort for us. We had to wait in the reception area, which consisted of a series of secure compartments, each one taking up to ten prisoners. They looked like cages to me, something like you might see animals in, at a zoo. Many of the men were smoking and the smell and the noise was horrific.

"Hey Guv! How long's this gonna take?"

"When do we get to the wings?"

"We've been here for hours! When you going to let us out?" The shouting and swearing went on, but there we had to stay for over two hours, with only a wooden bench to sit on. During that time they brought us round some cold pie and a cup of tea, but I was so weary and shaken up I just couldn't get it down.

The inhuman process continued when we were formally admitted. I was stripped and searched. My own clothes were put in a bag and taken away. I was allocated a cell on D wing, and by the time I was escorted there it was about 7.00 p.m. - association time.

"Hi there," I said wearily to my new room-mate, who was lying on his bed reading. He didn't respond, so I carried on, "I don't suppose you'll have to put up with me for long anyway; I've put my name down for a single cell, and hope to get one soon." It was only meant as a friendly greeting - the first thing I could think of. But it was definitely the wrong thing to say. He absolutely erupted off the bed; he went almost crazy; he cursed and swore and called me every name he could think of. I realised later, when he'd calmed down a bit, that every prisoner wants a cell to himself, and that he had had his name down for a single cell for months.

That night I slept with one eye open and the other shut. You can't be too careful, I thought to myself; after all, these days instead of putting people with mental problems in the proper institutions, they were sending them to prison. Unfortunately for me he was a smoker, and I really couldn't take the smoke. At nights he would block off the observation flap in the door and start smoking his pipe; well it wasn't really a pipe, it had tubes coming from it and he sucked it through a bucket of water. I hadn't seen such a contraption before, and have no idea what it was called; perhaps it was his own nameless invention. From the effect it had on him I should guess it was his way of imbibing drugs. It continually made a strange bubbling noise and gave out an offensive smell which made my eyes smart, but there was nothing I could do about it.

Next day I phoned Cheryl and told her to get together some of the brethren and pray. I needed a single cell fast. To my heart's delight she said she had already done just that and was having a prayer meeting that very night. Maybe that sounds very self-centred to some-one who has never been "inside". But in the noisy, crowded prison environment some degree of privacy was essential if you were to stay sane. Most prisoners would give anything for a bit of their own space. You wouldn't want to be locked up with some-one with mental problems, who may be violent, knowing that you couldn't just get up and walk away if the situation got out of hand. Two days later our prayers were answered. I was walking on the landing when I heard my name being called out. It was my cell-mate, he told me that he had a friend who had a single cell and if I wanted I could move in to it and the friend would move in with him. I didn't hesitate; I packed my things and moved in.

Life in Bullingdon was extremely harsh and rigorously regulated. Inmates were escorted by officers everywhere. If we were going to get meals or to the gym or the prison shop, going for exercise, or to the Chapel, in fact just about everywhere we went, we needed an approved escort to unlock the seemingly endless system of secure gates, and lock them behind us. The simplest journey became a mammoth exercise. And if no prison officer was available at that time, then we couldn't go. The food was still lousy and the signs of this were all over the walls. (Disgusted by it, the inmates threw it everywhere!) The days were filled with minor disturbances: fights would break out among the inmates; officers would rush to stop the fights; alarms sounded as officers summoned help from their colleagues; all this was punctuated by incessant swearing, and the use of drugs. It was the home of sin and the hospital of sorrows.

The nights were just as bad. They were long and lonely nights, and I often heard grown men crying for their wives and families. There were occasions when inmates would break up their furniture and take out their frustration on the door. Some were begging for mercy - why they were begging for mercy can only be left to the imagination. And there was the loud music which went on the whole night - try to imagine 100 different kinds of music playing at the same time and no means of telling anyone to turn it down. Some inmates had nothing to do at all during the day; some by choice, others because the available jobs and educational courses were very limited and given to a privileged few. This meant that many prisoners slept through the day and were wakeful at night. Cheryl managed to find me some sophisticated ear plugs made of wax, which had to be moulded to fit the ear. They worked well, they blotted out the noise and enabled me to sleep. But eventually she was stopped from bringing them in; the prison authorities said they created a safety hazard, as I would have been blissfully unaware if the fire alarm had sounded.

For most of the day I was locked up, as I didn't have a job and there was a waiting list for education. Eventually, as I mixed with the other men, word got to me that there was an inmate who made himself out to be a lawyer and that he was working on his own appeal. I was desperate to get out, so I quickly made his acquaintance and asked whether he could help me get my case back to the Appeal Court. (Suddenly I recalled Joseph, in the Old Testament, who, when he was in prison begged his fellow prisoner the Butler to bring his case before the king, when he was released.) The so-called lawyer said he was in the middle of doing his own case, but would do all he could to help. I handed over some of my papers to him, but thought I would wait to see how he got on with his own case.

Weeks later he went off to court. That day I waited anxiously, hoping to hear news. Late that afternoon I was in my cell and I heard a familiar voice in the corridor. I thought no, it can't be. Then there was a knock at the cell door.

"Come in", I said downheartedly. In walked the amateur lawyer. He dropped his belongings, shook his head and said,

"You'd better forget it, you're not going to get past those three judges; none of us is going anywhere." My heart sank and I felt gutted. All my hopes in him were dashed. Now I realised how devastated Joseph must have felt when he realised that the Butler had forgotten all about him as soon as he was out of the prison. No wonder the scripture says we are not to put our confidence or trust in any man.

That night as I lay in bed I thought a lot about the life of

Joseph, and his hard times. He knew what it was like to be wrongly accused by Potiphar's wife, and imprisoned for many years. He had no idea when he would be released, but worse still I could imagine the pain in his soul when he was left to languish after the Butler forgot his promise to him. But the scriptures said that God was with Joseph! My mind drifted to other Bible characters and the horrendous circumstances that God allowed to come into their lives. I thought of Shadrach, Meshach and Abednego in the middle of the burning fiery furnace; Daniel in the lion's den; the Apostle Paul lashed five times with 39 stripes, shipwrecked, pursued by bandits, stoned and left for dead. What did they think? What was going through their minds? How did they feel? Suppose they had said,

"Lord, why me? I can't take any more, this is too much. We were prepared to follow you, we were prepared to live for you, but we never expected this. We never realised it meant going through a burning fiery furnace heated seven times." What if Daniel had said,

"Lord they have been trying to kill me for years, and I can't go through any more." What about Paul? I would have understood if he had got up after the stoning and just told God that he had had enough. And what about the Master himself? There can be no doubt that his darkest hour was in the garden of Gethsemane, and then the agony of Calvary. I took comfort, and drifted into sleep knowing that the God who was with Joseph and the great giants of old was with me too.

I started attending the gym, and found that it helped to take my mind off my circumstances. It also gave me an opportunity to tell some of the other inmates about God. By now I was going to the chapel regularly. There were about 10 men attending. I had a chance to talk to the men and the officers, and eventually many began to bring their problems to me so that we could pray over them. There were all sorts of problems - parole, home leave, sickness, family problems, drug problems. The chapel was the one place where men from all the wings could mix freely together. Most only came for tea and biscuits; some came to hear about the Word of God; some came for counselling, and others used it as an excuse to meet up with men from the other wings.

Sadly, there were many inmates who looked constantly for ways of obtaining drugs. Many times on family visits I had observed drugs being surreptitiously handed over. Visitors might have it in their socks and then hand it over under the table. Then it would be carried back by the inmate secreted somewhere on his body.

Some of the inmates were also hoping that in the chapel they could get free cigarettes. The condition of the chapel sometimes grieved me. It was at this time that I met Bob, who was one of the teachers on the Multi-skill Computer course and he used to visit the chapel whenever he was working in the prison. He seemed quite excited when he first met me and found out that I was a Christian. He said there had always been a christian prisoner in Bullingdon, ready to speak out for God, right from the time it first opened. Dave, who had held this role in recent months, had just left. Bob assumed that God had called me to be His on-going witness in this place, because there was so much that could be done in the cells and on the wings by inmates, when chaplaincy staff were not available. From our first meeting he saw me as a called missionary, rather than a persecuted individual. He was a real 'Barnabas' - an encourager, a God send. He noticed how discouraged I was and he would often pray with me.

Eventually I spoke to the Chaplain and asked if I could have a prayer meeting in my cell. He agreed, but said I would have to get the final approval from the officer in charge of my landing. I was over the moon when the wing officer said yes. It seemed like a miracle. Normally you were not allowed to have more than a few people in a cell at a time. I desperately hoped that no-one would come who would wreck it. It was a great opportunity, but also a dangerous one. At first it was difficult to get anyone to attend, but after some weeks they began to trickle in, until the cell couldn't hold them. Some sat on the bed, one sat on the toilet, some brought in extra chairs and others leant against the sink. I was delighted with the overwhelming response, but at the same time I was apprehensive. I desperately wanted it to become a safe and standardised prayer meeting, and not get out of hand.

After a time I felt the Lord pointing out to me that one of the men was a spy. It seemed that he was sent to check if what we were doing was legitimate, or whether we were planning a break out. I was reminded of the spies who were sent to try Jesus by what he said to the people,

"Keeping a close watch on him, they sent spies who pretended to be honest."

I decided to tackle the matter head on,

"Would you like to lead the meeting in prayer, brother?" I asked. He glowered at me,

"You're a religious fanatic," he said as he hurriedly left the room; and that was the last prayer meeting he attended.

I also spoke with the Chaplain and got permission for the gospel choir from my church in Edmonton to come in and sing in the chapel every three months. From then on the chapel's membership grew dramatically. Soon numbers had tripled. Now it was standing room only! The men wanted to come to chapel more than before because services were different and exciting.

Christmas came, and it was the most miserable time I've ever spent. It should have been a happy occasion at home with my family, but instead I was spending it in a maximum security prison with 600 convicts. The food for once wasn't all that bad - roast beef, Yorkshire pudding, vegetables, ice cream and jelly. Not our usual pet food! Although I honestly believe that pet lovers fed their animals better food than we normally got. I remember once looking at the food on my tray. The gravy was transparent and turning to an officer I asked him if he recognised what it was. He replied that he had no idea what it could be either!

New Year's Eve arrived to the sound of much merrymaking. Many were busy making their hooch and getting ready for the celebrations. That night, as Big Ben struck midnight, just about every radio in the prison was turned on full blast. It was as if you were only inches away from the actual clock itself. Then everyone started shouting and there was a horrible noise of metal doors being simultaneously slammed. I looked back over the year and thanked God for His mercy. I was sure that God had a plan for me being where I was and I prayed that God would grant that I would fit in with that divine plan.

1994: Time slowly passed and there was still no news of my appeal, but by now Cheryl had told me that she and a few of the church members were getting together to set up a defence campaign to fight to clear my name. This cheered me up immensely and I hoped that they would at least try to put some pressure on the Court of Appeal to give me an early date.

One day I phoned home, as I sensed that something was wrong. My wife told me that she was having some problems with the children and she wasn't coping well. This threw me once more under a cloud of gloom. I knew how difficult it must be for Cheryl to discipline our growing children when she was on her own, especially now that the three girls were all teen-agers and Jonathan at 8 was at an age when he really needed his Dad. I couldn't do a thing to help and I sat in my cell and cried. It was one of the worst days of my sentence. Then I heard the voice of the Lord simply saying,

"Look outside." I forced back the tears and looked.

There, outside my cell, I saw the most awesome sight I have ever seen. There were horses with nostrils flaring (as if they had just finished a race), all lined up on the grass. My eyes went down towards their feet and started to work upwards. As I looked to see who their riders were, they vanished out of sight. I wondered if I was hallucinating, or maybe even going crazy. It did happen to people in prison, I knew. But no, I felt relief as several Bible verses came to mind. This was to be another turning point for me. God showed me that day that He would never leave me nor forsake me, and that the host of heaven was with me. As it says in the Psalm,

"For he shall give his angels charge over you, to keep you in all your ways."

One evening as I was preparing for my prayer meeting, I saw a group of guys sitting at the top of the stairs on the upper balcony and I suddenly decided to invite them to my prayer meeting. This was a category B wing, and these were long term prisoners. We all recognised them as a group of tough men, who liked to think that they were the top dogs of the wing. Their leader was the toughest of them all. They seemed unlikely candidates for a prayer meeting, but something made me call up to them,

"Hey! you guys! Would you like to come to my prayer meeting?" They laughed uproariously but made no other comment. The ring leader was sitting on the top of the stairs peeling an orange. It was amazing that while the rest of us were only allowed one orange and an apple per week, he had a whole box full! He got up to walk away, laughing and joking with his mates. Suddenly I heard a dull thud. I looked up to the upper landing and saw that the gang leader was on the ground; one of his cronies was looking down at him trying to laugh, but I could tell from his face and the strangled laugh that something was badly wrong. I rushed up the stairs and found the leader flat out and foaming at the mouth. I dropped to my knees beside him, and quickly and urgently prayed for him. He was completely unconscious and his chums shouted for medical help, but no doctor or nurse was immediately available. It was a Saturday evening and the whole wing erupted in a frenzy of concern, as everyone shouted for some-one to help him. I laid my hands on him, and prayed out loud, which frightened some of his friends.

"Get off him!" yelled one of them, "Leave him alone! It's nothing to do with you."

"Stand back," I said firmly, "This is something you don't understand, just let me get on with it." I continued to pray, while I wiped away the vomit from his face, and gradually, gradually he began to come round. I spoke quietly to him, and by the time the nurse arrived about ten minutes later, he was fully conscious. She took him to his cell where she checked him over and found him to be OK. Later, I asked him what had happened.

"I don't know mate; I just heard this noise in my head, like a buzzing sound, and that was it, I just hit the ground." He didn't know what had happened; I didn't know what had happened; but from then on there was a definite difference in the place, as far as I was concerned. For one thing the tough guys treated me with a new respect. I was even greeted with polite "Good mornings" instead of the snarls and jeers I had been used to. But the biggest difference was in the Gang Leader himself. For a start he was the first to arrive at my prayer meetings! He would always hurry to get there, then look around at my empty cell in surprise and say "Where is everyone?"

An amusing thing happened to me one night. As I sat writing, suddenly a flash of light went past my window. I stopped writing and wondered what it was. Could this be a visitation from God? I hoped that it was. I thought of Peter in prison and how the angel came and took him out, and I wondered if an angel was here to take me out too! But the light had disappeared. The next night the same thing happened and I quickly jumped up and opened the window. To my disappointment the 'visitation' was only other inmates swinging tin cans containing fire out of their windows. They passed the fire from cell to cell to each other, as this was their only means of lighting their cigarettes after "bang up"!

How I longed for God to come and get me out of this hell hole. Every time an officer passed my cell door I hoped that he was coming to tell me that I could go home and that they had found the real culprit.

At last I received the news I had been hoping for: that a date had been fixed for my appeal - 1st November 1994. Around this time I started to make enquiries also to move to a Category C prison. I felt an urge to move on. I thought that a C Cat. would be more flexible and have more facilities to do things during the day, and I hoped to get closer to my home and family.

Summer turned into Autumn and I looked forward to the appeal. I felt sure I was going home to my family. Around this time a new law was passed by the Home Office stating that prisoners could only have a limited amount of belongings in their cell. Officers stripped cells almost bare, which so incensed the men that it led to a riot. Inmates began burning their bedding and anything else they could get their hands on and started throwing them out of the windows. They broke up their furniture and there were riot police everywhere. It was a very frightening time and there was a total shutdown of movements. We had to make cups of tea using the hot water from the tap, as breakfast didn't arrive until 11.00 a.m. Dinner was late evening. Most of the inmates weren't even allowed to make any phone calls; the privileged few who were allowed to phone were restricted to two minutes; and we were "banged up" virtually all day for nearly two weeks. I prayed even more that God would hasten the day to the 1st November so I could get out of all this.

October 31st arrived, the day before the Appeal, and I spent the day saying farewell to all whom I had come in contact with in Bullingdon - inmates, officers and friends. Everyone was optimistic. As it was the tradition, I gave away all my groceries and whatever else the guys asked for. When 1st November came I was ready to go to the High Court. I looked at the cell which had been my home for the last 15 months. It was virtually bare.

"Best of luck, Millen," an officer said as I was escorted towards reception. There I signed some forms and two officers escorted me to a waiting cab. I was in an eager, optimistic frame of mind as I took my leave of HMP Bullingdon.

12

My Appeal to Justice

I remember very little of the hour's drive to London, to the Royal Courts of Justice in the Strand. I guess my mind was probably on what I would do if my appeal was successful. I had so many plans and ideas. I expected to see my family that day. Would the children be surprised when I went home with them, or were they expecting it too? I wondered if they had prepared any little surprises for me at home. Certainly, I thought, Cheryl would have my favourite meal ready.

When I arrived at the Appeal Court I was ushered downstairs to a holding cell which was in the basement. When I was called into Court I had to go up a narrow spiral staircase, which was so narrow that there was no room to pass on it. At the top of the stairs I entered directly into the dock, and I immediately saw the familiar faces of my family and the members of my church seated in the side gallery. When the three judges entered the court everyone was called to rise, until the judges had taken their seats.

The Judge started straight into the details of my case. He began by saying that 134 kilograms of cannabis had come into the country among the shipment which I had ordered from Jamaica. He told the Court about how Ralph and I had set up the business when we became redundant, and how we had had two earlier consignments from Jamaica with no problems. He said that the Customs check was a routine spot check, not as the result of a tip off, and that when the cannabis had been discovered, customs officers were placed to watch who unpacked the load. Well of course it was me and Ralph, and Len and Jim. But he only mentioned me and Ralph.

"It was noticed," said the Judge, "that the lighter cartons, which were those containing the cannabis, were set on one side." It sounded as though we were obviously expecting cannabis and were keen to get hold of it. I squirmed indignantly; because, of course, by the time we unpacked the truck the cartons didn't contain cannabis. They were empty. They were light. And of course we put them to one side - we had expected them to be full of ackees, and we needed to know what had happened to them. What would anyone expect us to do with empty tins in a valuable consignment?

The Judge explained to the Court how I had purchased the goods in Jamaica, but that a friend had taken the ackees to his own house before taking them for shipment. The Judge emphasised the fact that I had stayed in the same house as the ackees, in fact I had slept one night in the same room as the packaged ackees. He made a great point of the storage of the ackees. My friend had stated that it was my idea to store them at his house. But the Judge made it clear that I had always firmly denied that suggestion.

The court was told that there had been legal difficulties because Winston had never come to England, so could not be cross-examined. The Judge had to make it clear to the court that the case was legally sound, and he did so by referring back to another case some years before, which I knew nothing about. He seemed to be saying that even if Winston had known about the cannabis, and had helped to load it, that didn't make me any less guilty. He referred back to the summing up in my original trial in 1993 at Ipswich Crown Court, where the presiding Judge had said that whoever the drug smugglers were, they would not have sent the drugs to some-one who was not expecting them. It would have been too difficult for them to get hold of the smuggled drugs; so, as the whole consignment was addressed to me, I must have been expecting it; I must have known all about the drugs; I must be the guilty one.

The proceedings went on for the whole day, and my mind went from elation to despair and back again as something would be said by the Judge and I would think,

"Yes! Yes! That's just how it was! Now everyone can see the truth!" But a few minutes later my spirits would drop as it seemed that the evidence was against me. The Judge referred to the fact that the original jury did not seem to like the look of me, and that the summing up Judge, by pointing out to the jury that Ralph looked like a good living, innocent sort of fellow, might somehow have inferred that I didn't. The Judge considered whether this might have prejudiced my chances, but decided that it was fair after all, because the jury were quite capable of seeing for themselves what the defendants looked like.

At the end of that afternoon the three Judges failed the appeal, saying that such a huge quantity of drugs couldn't have been coming from Jamaica to no-one.

I was gutted. I was unable to move with shock. Despair once again rose up within me. It was all too hard to take in. I was numb.

"Oh, God," I thought "how much more of this can I take?" I was led back down the stairs, and I sat and waited.

About an hour and a half later I was on my way back to Bullingdon. It was all too hard to take in. How were my family and church members taking it? They had all been so positive that I was going back home on the van with them. And how was I going to face the inmates and officers who were convinced I wasn't coming back? I thought too of the riot which was still going on at the prison and how I had prayed to get out of it. Now I was going right back into it. My life was shattered and somehow I had to get hold of it and get it back onto the rails. I had to hold on firm to God.

As we drove back to Oxfordshire I looked at the two officers and the driver who were trying their best to console me, but I never heard a word they said.

I arrived back at Bullingdon and before long I was back on the wing. An inmate who was cleaning shouted out when he saw me, "The preacher man is back!" (Their nickname for me was preacher man). Then it started a chain reaction and everyone started to shout out, "The preacher man is back," from behind their closed doors. I know they were as gutted as I was.

I was allowed two minutes to telephone home. I learned that my home was in 'mourning'; I felt so very, very sorry for them. Inside in my cell I fell to my knees and sobbed my heart out. I asked God why, why was I taken back to prison? why couldn't I have gone home with my family? I didn't get an answer from God, but despite everything my life was in his hands. I had to go forward, forward through my hour of darkness. Then the familiar voice I knew so well spoke,

"Only rebel not ye against the Lord, neither fear ye the people of the land, for they are bread for us, their defence is departed from them, and the Lord is with us: fear them not."
They were comforting words and helped to take the misery out of my situation, but I didn't understand what God was trying to say to me. What next? It seemed as if this was absolutely the last straw; there were to be no more appeals. I felt totally washed up. Hope was fading, or so I thought. Where would I go from here?

13

Preacher Man at the Mount

I awoke on the 8th February 1995 with a feeling of excitement. My transfer to the Mount prison in Hemel Hempstead had been approved and this was to be my last day at HMP Bullingdon. I took a final look around what had been my home for 18 months, and I breathed a sigh of relief. These four grey walls had heard my crying out to God; they had seen my tears and my prayers. Now the cell was almost empty, as I once again had given away almost everything; only this time I knew for sure that I wasn't coming back. I had survived Bullingdon maximum security prison by the grace of God.

I thought of all the men I had come in contact with during my time in this prison. Men from all walks of life - doctors, solicitors, barristers - you name them and they are there. Then there are the violent top security convicts: drug addicts, murderers, robbers and the pimps to name but a few. I reflected on what I had seen in this place; the men who had come in as tough as old boots but had gradually been broken down before my eyes, eventually even asking for Bibles, and for me to pray for them. I had seen the many riots, the violence, so many examples of hatred and man's inhumanity to man. But I also thought of the many inmates who had come into contact with the Saviour, and whose bitter and twisted lives had been touched and changed by the power of God. I knew the truth of the words,

"A broken and a contrite heart, O God, you will not despise."

But now I felt in my heart that I was ready to move on. I had heard about life in the Mount: that it wasn't all that bad. It was said that the regime was easier, and besides - it was one more step closer to home.

After a hurried breakfast I was escorted to reception where there were the usual formalities and good-byes. I was ushered through the door inside the prison gates and into a waiting cab. This time there were no handcuffs. Soon we were heading down the Motorway and by afternoon we arrived in Hemel Hempstead. I was put again on an Induction Wing where I spent the next six weeks. It seemed that news of my transfer had reached The Mount before I did, because it wasn't long before the Chaplaincy Team, Pastor Williams and Ken Crighton came to greet me and give me a warm welcome. They told me that they had heard of the good work that God was doing through my life in Bullingdon, and that Bullingdon's loss was their gain.

The first thing that was evident on "Brister Wing" was that there was a lack of officers. It was not at all like Bullingdon. I was distressed to hear about the drug dealing that was going on; the muggings of prisoners by other prisoners, and the homosexuality. After six weeks I was transferred to a spur on "Lakes Wing". Here the guys left their cell doors open all day long without any fear of being 'burgled'. The understanding was that if anyone removed anything from another man's cell it meant certain death. So if you 'borrowed' something from someone's cell, you would make sure it was put back before night. The cons on this wing had heard of my conduct, and my belief in Christ, so I wasn't very much liked, and they didn't speak to me much. Sometimes as I walked past they would chant and sing for me to get off the wing, but that didn't bother me; calling me names couldn't hurt me at all.

I settled down the best I could, thinking of the day when I could put in for transfer to an open prison and my parole.

Better still was the hope that, with new evidence, I could get my case back to the Court of Appeal. I decided that however long it took, with the help of the Almighty God, I was not going to stop until my name was cleared.

The Mount allowed certain privileges, and one of them was cooking for myself, so I no longer had to endure prison cuisine. I also went back to my studies and decided to go in for Health and Social Care, First Aid, and Maths; after all I had some time to go before I was released. I began to help out in the chapel, and soon chapel services became better attended. I was given the chance to preach and once again Cheryl and some of the choir from Shiloh Church, Edmonton were allowed to visit once a month and sing at the services.

One day I noticed a new con on the wing, and my first thought as I gazed at him was, "What a mean looking brute!" He looked really evil and I did my best to avoid him. I would make sure that I did not have eye to eye contact with him because I was sure he would want to start trouble. One evening he walked in as I was taking a shower, and asked straight off,

"You the Pentecostal preacher I've heard so much about?"

"Yes," I admitted shakily; with only a towel for my defence I was understandably a little nervous.

"OK man. We gotta talk. I need to see you. OK?"

"OK," I agreed, getting out of the shower area as quickly as possible. Sure enough he returned to see me, as promised, in my cell a couple of days later. My heart pounded as I told him to come in. Then he began to tell me his background, explaining that he was a South American Muslim. Soon he started to pour out his heart, telling me that his girlfriend and child were in England seeking asylum and he wasn't there to help them and that his mother was going to have an operation for breast cancer back home. The distress was causing him to have a breakdown. Although he had seemed so menacing at first, I now realised that he was in need of help that I could not give him, nor any officer, or inmate, or any Chaplain. Only the Almighty could help him, and I prayed to the God of Heaven on his behalf. Nothing was impossible for Him to do. I pointed him to Christ and the way of Salvation and pretty soon he was coming to my cell more and more. We would discuss the scriptures and he would talk about the Koran. It wasn't long before he started coming to the chapel and eventually he committed his life to Christ. I watched as he stopped dealing in drugs, gave up smoking, cleaned himself up, got baptised and was on fire for God. Who could do that except God? As St Paul said,

"If any man be in Christ he is a new creature."

On another occasion a guy said he was desperate to talk to me, so I arranged to see him one afternoon at association time. He used to come to the chapel on and off, and showed quite a bit of interest, but he wasn't a committed Christian. That afternoon he told me the whole story; how some months earlier he had prayed to God when he had been in a very tight spot. Like so many others he had been in a drugs ring. He was a smuggler, smuggling drugs into the country. On one occasion he had swallowed a lot of drugs in plastic bags, expecting that they would eventually be passed out in the normal way. But this time they had got stuck somewhere and he realised that if something didn't happen soon, he would have to get to hospital quickly (which would certainly mean an operation and jail afterwards). Failing that he would need an undertaker.

In desperation he prayed, promising to mend his ways if only God would spare his life, and miraculously the packages passed through his body at the eleventh hour. He sold on the drugs, still intending to turn over a new leaf - but he promptly forgot his promise.

Now he was feeling guilty, as if God was somehow reminding him of his promise, and he really wanted to turn to God and go straight. I was able to pray with him, and he accepted the Lord into his life.

The seasons came and went and in May 1996 I was transferred to the "Hostel Wing" where we were allowed even more privileges. It was a wonderful improvement to my life-style. This wing was only for 30 of the most trusted inmates and no-one else. Here every prisoner had a key to his own cell, although the landing was always kept locked. We could go and come as we liked and there was no "banging up". We could go to bed when we wanted, and make as many phone calls as we wanted. Of course we were the envy of all the other prisoners, and every day we suffered a load of verbal abuse from the other inmates - not that we cared at all; compared to the rest of the prison system the Hostel Wing was like heaven.

After a while I grew weary of studying. I needed a break, and I applied for a routine job. I was allowed the job of cleaning the toilets, which wasn't quite what I had in mind, and which I detested. However, at least it gave me a chance to finish early and get back to my cell to read and study the scriptures. I cleaned those toilets with a passion, and soon even the officers stopped using their own loos and came over to ours.

"Hallo Tony!" they would call, in friendly greeting, as they came to use our toilets, "How you doing, mate?" Those hand basins sparkled. I even overheard the Maintenance Manager commenting that permission was not given for new hand basins to be installed! Other inmates asked if I was expecting a visit from the Queen! I had only been following the advice in the Bible:

"Whatsoever you do, do it heartily, as to the Lord and not unto men."

As I was making my way back to the wing from Education one day, I was stopped by a con who said he wanted to speak to me and show me something in the chapel. I followed him and when he got there he pointed to some murals on the wall.

"Look at that white Jesus, this is what you are worshipping, a white man! You're nothing but an Uncle Tom boy! I should kill you for spreading propaganda, I hate you and your doctrine." Years of bitterness and hostility showed in his face and I sensed straightaway that he was going to harm me. I decided to make my exit as quickly as possible and started to walk away, but he followed, cursing and saying that if he had a gun he would kill me. Just then I saw a group of Jamaicans, who heard me shouting at the con to leave me alone.

"What's happening Preacher man? Is this guy bothering you?" one of them called out; and to my attacker they shouted, "Leave the Preacher alone, man, or we'll cut you to pieces." And with that he walked away. I thanked God that He had made a way for me to escape, because for the first time I truly felt that my life was in real danger. I was too frightened at that moment to feel any compassion for the man, who acted as if he was crazy. It was really tragic, because I knew that this guy was a former Christian. It seemed that seven devils had really taken him over, as the scriptures warn.

After some time I was promoted to a top job, and with it went top wages of £10 a week! Two people out of the whole prison were needed to work in the Officers' Mess and I was asked to do it. I was allowed to walk unaccompanied through the main gates and across the car park (which was outside the prison) to prepare the officers' meals every day. My mind went back to the story of Joseph, in the Old Testament. I remembered how he was given favour in Egypt, and I thought how in my own situation I was trusted to prepare the officers' meals. But I was only trusted up to a point. I was still subject to the random strip search which I found such a great indignity. On one occasion I was returning to the gates when I was called aside, stripped and searched. So much for being trustworthy!

It may have been a good job; it may have been the best job in the prison; but, after a while, I felt that this was not the job for me and that God wanted me to move on to something else. I told the officers, and they couldn't understand why I wanted to leave such a cushy job. In the end they said I could work over on the new Induction Wing cleaning up rubbish. This was extremely unpleasant at times, as when the men threw bread out of their windows and it got wet, it was difficult to pick up. Some of the men who didn't like me excreted on pieces of paper and threw it out of the window for me to clean up. I wondered why God wanted me there, and I soon found out. The new convicts were locked up for most of the day and they were lonely. They had nothing to do, and no-one to talk to. Many of them spent their time looking through their windows all day long. This gave me the perfect opportunity to witness about Christ; and they had no choice but to listen. Once again they would share their domestic problems with me. I was able to pray with them, console them and encourage them not to take things too much to heart; assuring them there was still some hope. Eventually out of this, a Wednesday night service and Bible study started on that same Induction Wing. I marvelled at the truth of the words,

"The Lord does work in mysterious ways his wonders to perform."

The months drew on and when I put in for a transfer to Latchmere House Open Prison I was told there was a good chance of me going there - about 98%. This was a great thing for me to look forward to, and not only me, but Cheryl and the family as well. Latchmere was situated in Richmond Park, only 15 miles from our home in Edmonton. I would be able to go home for visits. Home! Home to be with Cheryl and our kids! Home to tuck into Cheryl's cooking again; to have a civilised shower; to watch tv with my family. I would be able to fulfil a meaningful role again in the church of which I was still nominally the Pastor. Also, at Latchmere House, I would be able to have a proper "outside" job, with ordinary people, and sensible wages. I would be able to contribute to the upkeep of my family again. OK, so it wouldn't be freedom; it wouldn't be the repeal of my sentence that I was still hoping for; but a move to Latchmere House would mean a much better life for me and my family, and Boy! was I hoping to go there!

About 2 p.m. one Wednesday afternoon I was in my cell reading when I heard the guys outside shouting,

"Spin! Spin!" To those in the know, this indicated that there was going to be a cell search. I heard dogs barking and officers telling everyone to move into the dining area. I made my way along with the others and left my door open. Some of the guys were in front of me, some tailed along behind. After the search we were told we could go back to our cells. As I walked back an officer said,

"Not you Millen, come with us." He took me to the office and closed the door.

"We found this in your cell," he said, holding up a small plastic bag containing a black substance.

"That's impossible!" I said, "you couldn't have."

"That's what we said too," came the reply. "We couldn't believe it either." I looked on in total disbelief.

"Anyone who's done this to me will pay for it, God will see to it," I said. My heart sank and my stomach turned over - devastation took hold of me. I couldn't believe what was happening. I couldn't think clearly. Here I was already fighting a drugs charge, of which I denied all knowledge, and here they were telling me they had found drugs in my cell. Rage began to well up in me and I decided I was not going to take it lightly. I was not going to be naive this time. This time I would call a solicitor straight away.

They took me down to solitary confinement. They took

away my job and stripped me of all privileges. But God was with me (just as He had been with Joseph,) and the Governor sent me back to my wing. Straightaway I phoned Cheryl and told her what had happened. I told her to get some members of my church together and pray. I learnt later that Cheryl had put the whole family on a prayer-fast, even my nine year old son Jonathan.

That night I even forgot to eat my dinner. All sorts of things raced through my head. How could a thing like this happen? Of course it was a "stitch up" once again. I thought of my conviction and sentence, and how God had used me throughout the prison system to bring comfort to others. I thought of my integrity before all the men; and now what were they to believe? They knew what I stood for.

I prayed to God and told him that He had to get me out of this - too much was at stake. All that had been built up would come tumbling down, and Satan would have the last laugh.

The next day, to my delight, the majority of the prison population had come out on my side. They were in a rage just like myself and they wrote to the Governor to let him know. Even the Chaplains had a conference and went to see the Governor. I called a solicitor, but an officer told me that they were going to carry out their own internal investigation. God was on my side, because a few days later I was called to the office and told that their investigations had been completed and (thanks be to God) they found the real culprit. It seems that someone who didn't like me and wanted to spoil my chances of getting to Latchmere House threw the drugs in as he was walking past my cell door. In my relief I thought of the words,

"Many are the afflictions of the righteous, but the Lord delivereth him out of them all."

The whole episode was another bad experience for me, but I thank God that the outcome was a sign of things to come. He had delivered me from the small one and He will deliver me from the big one to come. Before long everything was back to normal, and my transfer to Latchmere House was approved. November came and Cheryl came to meet me and travel with me to Richmond.

All my belongings were given to me and I was escorted to the main prison gates where the officer wished me good luck. It was the most wonderful feeling walking through those gates. The sound of birds singing had never sounded so sweet, and the crisp cold air had never felt so good, but best of all Cheryl was there waiting for me.

As we drove away I looked back and thanked God for keeping me for the past year and a half; I thanked Him for all the guys I had helped to counsel and point in the direction of Christ. I thought of a young man, a 'drug head', whom the Chaplain had asked me to talk to. When his first child had died, he had tried to end his life. Worse still his second child was badly sick in hospital and he had tried again to commit suicide. I told him he needed help to come off the drugs and advised him to go back to the rehab. unit at HMP Bullingdon. When he came back some time later he was off hard drugs and accepted the Lord Jesus into his life, to my delight. Soon after, when he went to the Court of Appeal, his sentence was so reduced that he was immediately released. He wrote to the Chaplain not long after and told him that he had been baptised and was going on with Christ. It was things like this that kept me going - to see what had been achieved for the glory of God.

I reflected back also to the time I had spent on Lakes Wing, where the guys had disliked me so much when I first arrived. Now many of them had come to know the Lord and were sad to know that I was leaving. It seems strange now to look back down the corridor of time and see how far I had come. When I entered The Mount I had no way of knowing whether I would come through the ordeal; at that time I felt that it was only by the Grace of God that I was still in my right mind.

We took the train to Latchmere. I could never imagine that it would feel so good to travel on a train. I never thought that a train ride would be so enjoyable. As I looked through the windows I noticed how everything looked different. The streets seemed to be chock-a-block with cars; people were rushing everywhere. It seemed that I was coming back to the real world.

14

Living on a Knife Edge
Latchmere House

When Cheryl and I arrived at Richmond station we took a cab and drove through Richmond Park. How beautiful it was; just watching the deer eating grass was a comfort. I felt so good.

As we arrived at Latchmere House, at the edge of the park, my idea of an open prison was shattered. My impression had been that you could go in and out as you pleased, but it was not so. The place was totally enclosed by high wire fences all around; just like all the other prisons before, and my heart sank. All the feeling of elation was wiped out in a minute. I said goodbye to Cheryl and rang the bell at the gate. A rather short, middle aged man walked slowly outside to open it and I gave him my name. He showed me to reception and told me,

"It'll be some time before you can be seen, mate, everyone's at lunch."

When at last I was seen to, there were the usual formalities - I was photographed, there were papers to fill out, and then I was sent to pick up my kit. I was given a key and allocated a cell on the Induction Wing, just like before. I was pleased about one thing that was the same as The Mount: there was no "banging up", and you could come and go on the wing as you pleased.

I looked around and observed that the men here seemed to be very busy going about doing their work, and they seemed to be kinder and more friendly. I went back to my cell and started cleaning. I had lost count of how many cells I had cleaned since my original incarceration. Nevertheless I spent the rest of that afternoon sorting out my new accommodation. I felt much better within myself and felt that the "furnace" that God was allowing me to go through was at last going out.

I spent the rest of that week in Induction classes. We went through a long list of do's and don'ts and were instructed in detail as to what the prison authorities expected of us. Latchmere was a drugs free, alcohol free, violence free environment, and to break any of their rules meant going back to a closed prison. This was the last thing the men wanted, and they did everything they possibly could to co-operate with the officers. It was a fairly small prison with about 130 inmates; many of these must have been professional people, judging by the type of cars their visitors arrived in. It was similar to the Mount with its cells and corridors, but with more generous facilities. There was a canteen for us to eat in, but many men still took their food back to their cells. There were gardens that we could walk in, which meant there was more for us to look at. The cells still had the observation window so that officers could check on prisoners without opening the cell door. The wing was locked at night, and if we were working outside we had to be back by 10.00 p.m.

The week went quickly by and what a contrast it was to the previous weeks. To earn extra hours on home visits you had to volunteer to do odd jobs in and around the prison, and I worked jolly hard for those extra two hours. I cleaned and scrubbed floors like never before.

When the weekend came I had my first visit from Cheryl; she came with the children, her mum and her brother Raymond. It was their first visit and it was to be their last, because at Latchmere there are no prison visits, only town and home visits. After a midday lunch and introduction to prison staff we were allowed to go into the town. We took the bus to Kingston town centre and it was such a joy to go freely where I wanted, without being told where to go, what to do, and when to do it.

We wandered through the stores and Cheryl's mum even treated me to some new clothes. Outside in the streets people were hustling and bustling around, which made a big contrast for me to the prison where everybody moved slowly. After some more lunch, I decided to go back to the prison a bit earlier than the time stated. In no way did I want to arrive back late - we had been warned enough times.

"You OK Millen?" an officer asked, when I got back. "Not feeling too good?"

"I'm fine," I said cheerfully, "Never felt better. Why?"

"I just wondered what had happened," he said "when I saw you back so early."

"Nothing's happened," I replied, "but it's better to be safe than sorry." We both laughed when he said he had never seen anyone coming back so soon after a town visit.

Back in my cell, I lay down on my bed and gave God thanks for a truly wonderful day. It had seemed like a dream and I knew that from this time onwards it could only get better and better.

A couple of weeks later, my first chance for a home visit came. That Saturday morning I jumped out of bed. I was going home! I couldn't believe it. I was so excited I started to sing; I don't think that a nightingale could have sung any sweeter! I changed into the new track suit that Cheryl's mum had bought me and headed down to reception. The reception area was full of excited cons laughing and joking. The cigarette smoke that filled the room made my eyes burn, but that morning I couldn't have cared less. I knew how they felt; they were looking forward to going home. When the door opened everyone rushed to join the queue to pick up their ID card. Every minute and every second counted. I hurried to the gate where Cheryl was waiting for me in the car; we headed down the A406 and within 45 minutes we were home.

I entered my house for the first time in over 3 years. It couldn't really sink in. I stood for a moment unable to take it in. The children welcomed me with beaming smiles and hugs and kisses and there were a few relatives and friends there to greet me. We spent the rest of the day just chatting and laughing and eating some real good home cooking. That afternoon I left early for Latchmere with Cheryl driving me in the car, but the journey back didn't go too well. We got stuck in traffic and I sat nervously; my heart pounding, wondering whether I would make it back in time. Officially, we were required by prison rules to return to the prison by public transport, so that any delay could be verified. If your bus got stuck in a traffic jam, or the train broke down, you were OK. But if you turned up late and they found you had been travelling in your wife's car you would be in real trouble. "Please God, clear the traffic for us", I begged. God heard and answered and I arrived back in time. It was one of the happiest days of my life and I thanked God for his goodness.

Within a few months I got a job on the outside, working for a bed distribution company. It meant that now I was out of the prison from 8 a.m. until 10 p.m. What a blessing it was. I received my first wage packet, out of which I had to pay my "rent" at Latchmere. Then they would deduct a certain amount to be put by for my savings, which was a good idea, because most cons didn't have a thing to go home with, let alone any money.

Things were slowly getting back to normal, but I was longing for the day of my parole - 1st August 1997. I had heard from other inmates that if you show remorse for the crime you have been imprisoned for then you are more likely to get parole; but if you continue to deny it, then there would be no chance of parole. I tried not to think about it, because there was no way I was going to admit to something I had not done, even if I had to serve my time all over again. I was not guilty.

Every Sunday evening I would rush off to join the guys in the chapel for the service. When I first started to go, it consisted only of biscuits and tea, general chit-chat, a closing prayer by Fred Spurrier the Chaplain and back to the cells. Cakes were brought in by Fred's wife and her friend, and it was a blessing for the men. Fred was a blessing for me also. Every Saturday he would come to my cell and pray with me. He cared deeply for the men and hoped that they would change for the better. As time passed on I felt something was missing in the chapel services and I thought more emphasis should be put on the spiritual side of things. I mentioned it to Fred, and he said I could go ahead and implement some changes if I wished, and that he would always be at hand to make sure everything was OK.

I set about getting the guys together, and teaching them some new choruses. I got some of them to play on the instruments - and we had a church! What a difference it made. Every Sunday more and more men kept coming, and even the officers, when they heard the singing, came round to see what was going on. Soon I started a mid-week prayer meeting where the men brought their problems and asked that we prayed for them. Many lives were touched by God, and many guys who had given up on God found their faith in Him once again. One of them, who learned to play an instrument for the chapel in Latchmere now plays regularly in his own home church. In the end the room got too small and the plan was to ask the Governor for a bigger place. Praise God! (But sadly I left before it was realised).

The months dragged on and sometime in March my case came before the Parole Board. The woman officer from the board explained a few things and asked if I was still maintaining my innocence.

"Yes, I certainly am," I said. "Even if I have to stay in here for another eight years, I will always deny the charge. I'm not guilty."

"What's your view on drugs?" was her next question, and when I had dealt with that to the best of my ability, she continued,

"So, why did you attend the Drugs Awareness Course at the Mount?" I explained that it was so that I could help other people to come off drugs.

"And how do you feel about other people using them?" she asked. The questions went on and on, until it seemed almost like another court case.

"Well, don't bank your hopes on parole this time Mr Millen," she said at last, "but we will let you know the outcome within the next few weeks."

"OK; fine," I said, "I look forward to hearing from you." She had clearly wanted me to show remorse, but how could I show remorse for something I never did?

I returned to work, but all I could think of was the interview and how it went. I wondered how many people might have been locked up innocently and then had admitted to guilt just so that they could go home. It was so unjust and so unfair.

About the middle of July I was called to the phone while I was at work. It was the probation officer at the prison. I guessed it was probably a spot-check, making sure that prisoners were all in their allocated work places. I hoped it wasn't anything more serious; I hoped she wasn't going to call me straight back to the prison, or tell me that I couldn't have that job any more.

"I have good news for you Mr. Millen," she said, to my surprise, "your parole has been approved and you will be released on 1st August." Well! I could have dropped to my knees then and there and worshipped God, but I decided I would leave it till later. The guys who I was working with didn't know I was in prison (only the Manager knew), and they would wonder why I was acting so strange. I phoned Cheryl straight away and told her the news. In two weeks I would be home for good. I could hardly speak. God was so good. I have heard of so many prisoners who do not get parole if they continue to insist on their innocence, but apparently I had a good report from the probation officer, and the chaplain at the Mount had reported on how many men I had persuaded to come off drugs.

As the 1st August drew closer I started bringing my belongings home. 31st July arrived and during that day I was summoned to see my probation officer for a final interview. She went over the discharge formalities and told me to report to my new probation officer the following day. That evening the guys all came to my cell one by one wishing me all the best.

"You deserve to go home, Tony," some of them assured me, "if anyone deserved to go home, you do." I wished them all well and begged them to keep themselves out of trouble. I recollected the good times I had spent in the chapel, and I thought of the many men who had really tried to behave themselves, but temptation had overcome them and they found themselves back in a closed environment. That reminded me of one guy who was caught for taking drugs, and the fear of being sent back to a closed prison made him try to jump over the fence, but he fell and broke his legs. I gave away everything that was left (as was the usual practice) and said my goodbyes once again, like so many times before. But this time I wasn't going to another prison - I was going home.

I had a sleepless night, tossing and turning and wishing for the morning to come. When at last it did come, it seemed like the longest morning of my life! I just wanted to rush off home, but first there were all the formalities to see to. There were official papers to be signed; I had to fold up my bedding and empty my cell. The whole process seemed so slow, especially as I knew Cheryl would be waiting, just the other side of the gate, but I couldn't get to her. At reception I saw the other men going out to work as usual, and I couldn't help noticing how enviously they looked at me, wishing that they too were going home. At last I was cleared by security, given my savings and a few extra pounds for good measure.

"Goodbye everyone!" I shouted, and stepped through the gates to freedom. I turned and looked back at Latchmere for the last time, as we drove away. It had been like living on a knife's edge and I was so glad it was all over. Now I vowed I was going to do everything I could to clear my name, with God's help.

15

Cheryl's Story

Right from the start, from the moment the red-haired customs officer had put the handcuffs on me, I had been determined to let everyone know that I was innocent of this crime of which I was being accused, and for which I was later convicted and imprisoned. It was very important for me, my family and my church to prove my innocence. But while I was in prison, the burden of trying to prove my innocence fell on Cheryl. She never gave up; she never let me down. She kept going, past the point of exhaustion, and so it seems appropriate here to have her tell in her own words about the fight to clear my name.

It was 1st November 1994, and I was at the Court of Appeal with a group of my family, and friends from our church. As we sat and waited for the others to arrive we felt confident that Tony was coming home with us that day. I knew that lots of people were coming, and sure enough the small room was soon full. I glanced around and saw friends, relatives and colleagues. We saw Tony being escorted in, then we were told to rise and the three judges walked in.

At that point everything from the first trial came rushing back into my mind. Once again our lives it seemed rested in the hands of those Judges, and I prayed to God that this would be the last time we would ever again see a Judge.

For the whole morning our QC outlined the

necessary points of the case, and in the afternoon Customs did theirs. Then came the verdict:

"The conclusion is that all grounds of the Appeal fail and the Appeal is accordingly dismissed." I heard one of the Judges say, and with that they got up and walked away.

I sat in total disbelief at what I heard. It couldn't be true. Now everyone would believe that Tony was guilty. We all sat in silence for some time looking at each other and wondering if we had heard right. I turned to Jennifer, sitting next to me, and asked her if she had heard the same thing as I had . Was this it? As the Judges walked away they had seemed to me to be completely cold and heartless; I knew that they could have let Tony go if they had wanted. We had been told that the case had a 50/50 chance of success. As I looked around at everyone, there were some with tears streaming down their faces once again - just like the first trial. Once more I watched heartbroken as Tony was led away.

We came out and my only comfort was to speak with our barrister. I asked him what we could do now. It seemed as if this was it. It was all over and all our efforts had failed. To my surprise he gave a glimmer of hope: he said that if we could find some new evidence we would stand a good chance of bringing the case back to court. He explained what we had to do and warned me that it would not be easy, but as he left he said,

"I have a funny feeling I'm going to see you all again."

We returned home in total silence; everyone locked in their own thoughts. Once again I was returning home without Tony. The children had put up Welcome Home banners, but when they did not see their Dad, they tore them down. It was heartbreaking to tell them all over again that their father wasn't coming and that he would have to serve his sentence.

The friends who had supported us at the court came back home with me. We all sat in silence unable to say anything - a bit like Job and his friends, in the Bible. I was devastated; the whole family was devastated; our friends were devastated. We sobbed our hearts out.

It was a cold evening and I was totally worn out mentally and physically. My head was spinning. I was in a daze. Although I wasn't physically in prison, I felt that my mind was locked in one. Eventually I went out alone in the dark. I just had to get away from everybody and talk with God. I needed to know where He was all this time and why He didn't answer our cries for help. But there was no answer. As I looked up at the stars there was only the tempter's voice saying God hated us and had abandoned us. But the devil was a liar, and I continued to talk to God.

"Have you forsaken us?" I asked. "Your Word says that you will never leave us nor forsake us, but I really feel forsaken right now."

There was nothing but silence. I told Him that I felt like an animal caught in a trap, but there was no-one to get me out. I told Him He was doing nothing to help and that our cries were falling on deaf ears. At one point I told the Lord that it was pointless reading the Bible and praying because He just ignored me. Why bother. It was as if He had just turned His back on me and was hearing and helping other people and not us. I even sang to Him,

> *"Pass me not O gentle Saviour,*
> *Hear my humble cry,*
> *Whilst on others thou art calling,*
> *Do not pass me by,"*

hoping that it might help the situation, but that didn't work either. I said many things that I shouldn't have said, and in the end I had to repent.

My mind reflected on Job of the Bible. He also said many things that he shouldn't have said. Even Habakkuk, prophet of the Lord, accused God of not hearing him. I felt just like them and I knew how Joseph must have felt when he was thrown into prison. I felt like a lot of God's people in the Bible must have felt, when they thought that they were forsaken by Him. I could now identify with them. Suddenly the stories in the Bible were not just tales of a long time ago; they were real, and some of the things that those people went through were now happening to me.

*I felt that I couldn't take any more and I wondered how long I could go on. God said in His word that He would not give us more trials than we could bear and I brought my strong reasoning to God asking Him as to how much more **He** thought I could bear, because **I** couldn't bear any more. But there was not a word. I contemplated walking off into the night and not coming back. But I couldn't; I had to remain strong, for myself, for Tony and for the children. They were all depending on me.*

For the next three days darkness just seemed to cover us and I wondered where God was and if he cared at all. For a passing moment my mind flashed to Mary and Martha when Lazarus their brother died - how they had called for Jesus to come, but He turned up when Lazarus was already dead and buried. I knew how they must have been feeling - completely gutted. But just like Martha and Mary, on the third day we too had a wonderful breakthrough.

I was at home sitting on the sofa, going over in my mind what steps I should take next when there was a knock at the door. It was Jennifer, Tony's cousin. A little while later there was another knock. It was a neighbour. They could see the devastation I was going through. They tried to cheer me up and asked what could be done with regards to Tony's case. I explained to them what the Barrister had said about getting new evidence, and how I had spent the entire morning phoning private investigators, hoping to find some-one who would be willing to take on Tony's case. But none of them wanted to get involved.

"You're talking about drugs, and you're talking about Jamaica; we wouldn't touch it with a barge pole, love," said one man. Discouraged, I then phoned Scotland Yard to see what advice they could give, but they also were unable to help.

"Well then," said my neighbour, when I had told them both of my lack of success, "we'll just have to try and get the information we need by ourselves." I looked at her. What I was saying about the difficulty of getting information didn't seem to be registering. I repeated what I had said, and pointed out that no-one wanted to take on the case because it was too dangerous.

"Let's still try and see what we come up with," she said again. "Nothing ventured, nothing gained."

"OK," I said, "you can use the phone yourself." She took the phone, checked out a number and telephoned, and to our utter amazement the information which we so badly needed, and which detectives thought would be impossible to get, was blurted out over the phone in less than a minute. This was nothing less than a miracle.

Suddenly it was like a heavy load lifted off my shoulders and the light of life came shining through. Weeping had endured for a night, but joy sure came that morning. We were over the moon. Hope had returned. I felt like how Martha had felt when her brother walked out of the tomb. Jesus had walked into our 'tomb' and rolled away the stone.

Armed with the information, we now had to search hard to find investigators who might be willing to take on the case. Through a close friend we enlisted the help of a detective and we asked him whether he thought it was still possible to gather information after such a long time. He took away our papers to look at and when he got back to us a few weeks later he said he believed it was possible, but they would have to go to Jamaica to find the evidence. Then came the shock: their fees would be £28,000! Our spirits crumpled. How could they ask so much? Where in the world would we get that sort of money? There was only one thing to do: we had to pray, and pray we did.

It was then that a few of us decided that we should form a committee to fight to clear Tony's name. We would call it the Free Anthony Millen Campaign. We prayed and asked God for direction and it soon became clear that somehow we had to trust God to help us find the money. To our astonishment the detectives said that they would help us by accepting payment by instalments, and they further reduced the cost by £10,000. We immediately set about fund-raising to raise the cash.

Our first fund-raising was to be a gospel concert. It was the only thing we could think of that would raise a substantial amount of money in one effort. It was something we had never done before, but we were going to have a go. We wrote to a few gospel artists explaining our plight and some of them agreed to help us free of charge. We blessed God. Everyone worked extremely hard to put it together; friends and supporters advertised the event widely, sold tickets, cooked and prepared food for the buffet refreshments, and got the church ready for the big event. The performers rehearsed carefully and gave of their best. On the evening the floor shook to the beat of the music; everyone seemed to enjoy it and we raised about £2,000. We needed at least £4,000 before we could send the detectives on their way. So we borrowed another £2,000 and the detectives left for Jamaica two weeks later.

Although the effort of organising the concert had almost exhausted me, as soon as it was over we had to set to work to plan our next event - a three course dinner. At the same time the committee decided that we should get MPs and newspapers involved. We needed to get the case publicised - this was a miscarriage of justice and everyone should know about it. We contacted Bernie Grant, MP and were delighted when he agreed to give whatever assistance we needed. We also set about getting petitions signed and taking them to the Home Office. Next we arranged newspaper and radio interviews - we did everything we could to keep the story alive.

The committee worked incredibly hard, day after day and sometimes late into the night to get things done. We went backwards and forwards to solicitors, meetings and interviews and there were times when we really felt it was becoming too much. Committee members dropped out one after the other, but we had others who would quickly fill their place. I myself found it extremely hard to concentrate on anything. Although Tony was the one behind bars, sometimes I felt that I was living in a prison as well. My thoughts were constantly on him and how he was coping. I visited him every week, which involved quite a bit of juggling of family commitments. At times I found it hard to cope with everything: bringing the family up on my own, the arrears on the house mortgage and the criticisms which I received from some people both inside and outside the church. There were people who thought that Tony might be guilty and that I was trying to shield him. But I had to soldier on and hold my head up high; we had done nothing to be ashamed of. It would have been so easy to have given up and thrown the towel in, but for Tony's sake we had to go on. I gained courage from thinking of other innocent prisoners, whose families and friends never gave up on them, and who finally brought about their release.

After the investigators had returned from Jamaica we met with our solicitor and gave him our findings. In May 1997 the case was sent off to the Criminal Cases Review Commission for the next hurdle. We never gave up praying.

We arranged fund raising after fund raising. We had more concerts and more dinners and made endless appeals for funds.

It was a tremendous relief for me when Tony came home on parole in August 1997. Suddenly the heavy load of fund raising became easier for me to bear, because he was there to share it. Life slowly got back to normal and at last it seemed like the 'heat of the furnace' was cooling down.

I had heard some inspiring sermons on the 'Testing of Your Faith', but never imagined that it would happen to us. Like other catastrophes in life, it happened to other people, but not to you. A preacher once said that pain, heartache and failure come to make us strong. It all began to make sense now. Now I understand when God says that He will be with us when we pass through the waters, that they will not overflow us; and that when we walk through the fire we will not be burned. I have come to realise that the 'fire of testing' is hot - really hot. Now I can also say that it doesn't make sense ranting and raving and trying to wriggle your way out of it; God will keep you in the situation you are going through until the time is right for Him to take you out. He has something definite in mind, but it may take some time to find this out. He's in the business of making us more like His Son, and in the process He may chasten us. There is no escape. We must get it into our heads that we will not get to heaven on a bed of ease. The Apostle Paul bore the 'brand marks' of his faith, so who are we to question God's testing? We are not more special than those who have gone before us. Some of us will go through maximum testing, we might lose all perhaps, but in the pain of life we shouldn't 'cast away our confidence', God will come through like He promised.

Although it might feel at times that God is nowhere to be found, He is right there with us.

"Lo, I am with you always, even to the end of the world", and He really does mean it. There was a time when Tony was in the prison and one particular day when I was at home it all became too much to bear. I cried my eyes out and told the Lord that if Tony was here I wouldn't be in the situation I was going through. Just as I finished speaking, the phone rang. I answered it trying to hide my anguish. At the other end was Tony. He explained that the Lord had told him to phone home to find out how I was. I thanked the Lord for seeing what was going on, and after the phone call I was able to pick myself up and carry on.

I remember another time when my son was giving me problems and in desperation I told him that if he didn't do what I told him to do, then his Dad would phone any minute and he would really be in trouble. That instant the phone rang. It was Tony and all he said was,

"Put Jonathan on the phone right now." He didn't even say hello, or how are you. The phone nearly fell out of my hand, and I thought "God you are awesome." God was letting me know that He was right there with me, keeping and strengthening me although I had thought otherwise.

The fund-raising continued until we had pretty much exhausted all the avenues for funds and just didn't know what to do next, when a good friend stepped in and gave us a substantial amount of money towards our costs. Now we needed only one more function to finally pay off our debts to the private investigators.

At last, in November 1998, we heard from the Criminal Cases Review Commission. When the phone call came it was Tony who answered.

"I have some good news for you Mr Millen," he heard, "I am pleased to tell you your case is going back to the Court of Appeal." With tears streaming down his face Tony fell on his knees just thanking God. We praised God, we danced, we sang, we jumped up and down. We just couldn't contain ourselves; we had to ring everyone and tell them the good news. Thank God we had not given up.

That night I found it hard to fall asleep. I kept thinking about the goodness of God. How He had been there all the time when I accused Him of not being there, and not answering my prayers when I wanted Him to. I thought of how He had re-opened the doors which had been closed, and had given us another chance. When it seemed that the case had come to a dead end, God gave us a good hope. We didn't believe for a minute that He had brought us this far to leave us.

"Verily God hath heard me, He hath attended to the voice of my prayer".

16

Free to Serve

As I write this chapter, I am still waiting for an appeal date, believing that God will vindicate me from a crime I did not commit, and a punishment I did not deserve. The four years I served in Her Majesty's Prisons will never go from my memory. They have made a lasting blot on my life and the life of my family. At least I know that they were not wasted years. I continue to hear the good news that former inmates still remember the "West Indian" who preached to them, and because of that they are now themselves born again. To God be the glory. If it was for just one soul, then the four years would have been worth it.

To have my freedom again and to take up the threads of my life is indeed very sweet. But for me, as for all returning prisoners or travellers, it was not as easy as I had anticipated. Fitting in at home took some time. Cheryl and the children had been getting on with life. They had learned to cope. Cheryl had been organising the family and paying the bills and here I was taking things over as if I had not been away. I think the biggest damage done was between myself and Jonathan. He had been "the man of the house" for four years and he resented it when I came back reclaiming my position. He was then eleven years old, and we just couldn't seem to understand each other. We had grown apart over those four years when I had seen him just once a week. I can now understand that when inmates come home after a long prison term, their families may have moved on with life and they can no longer fit it. If they don't give it enough time the relationship may break up irretrievably. Happily for us, we had much love and patience and knew that everything was in God's hands.

Life is slowly getting back to normal and Cheryl and the children are all doing well. I am back pastoring our local congregation of Shiloh Church, Edmonton. Looking back, perhaps I should have waited before taking on the task of leading the church. It was all too soon; but as I came out of the prison I was fired with a vision of what could be done in this small church. Ideas were tumbling round in my head of services, missions, outreach to prisons, work with young people and children, and care of the elderly in our area. If God was willing, we would build on what we had and venture out into new and exciting paths. I just couldn't wait to get started! So when in 1998 the leader of the Shiloh Fellowship and the Edmonton members said they would like to see me resume the position as pastor, I rose to the challenge. At that time the congregation were meeting in a small community hall. The first Sunday I was back it was crowded, with people standing in the aisles and outside in the corridors. The following Sundays it was still crowded, and we did not have the facilities for our large Sunday School. I decided that larger premises were required and we started worshipping in the Baptist Church in Edmonton, when it was not required by their own congregation. A steady growth continued and leaders were selected to start new activities.

My dream that our church should serve the community began to take shape. A Saturday School was started, offering extra tuition to local children and a place to do their homework. Our Praise and Worship team goes every month to sing at The Mount prison; I know how much this must be appreciated by the inmates, but I am not allowed by prison regulations to go with them! Preparations are in hand to provide a nursery, and a luncheon club for the elderly. We are involved, with the Baptist Church, in the European Urban Regeneration Programme in Edmonton. There are many gifts and abilities in our congregation. I believe they just needed some-one to inspire and lead them, and so I gave up the job which I had been doing while still in Latchmere House and threw myself into being a pastor. At the moment I have a dream of purpose built premises for our growing church and all its activities. Where the Master leads I will follow.

I have seen the light shine again after a time of great darkness in my own life, and this book is written to encourage and strengthen anyone who may be going through a time of darkness. Let me say that dark hours will come your way no matter how spiritual you are and how faithful to God you are. Suddenly, one day when everything is going well, tragedy strikes and your whole world comes tumbling down like a pack of cards. Christianity does not always remove the setbacks and tragedies of life, but the remedy lies in the Word of God. Whatever the situation is, it is not the end. It's not over even when it's over!

Nothing God allows in our lives is for our destruction. It's for our benefit. Sometimes He will lead us in ways that are beyond our understanding. He doesn't always explain the pathway that will sometimes take us through trials and pain; but rest assured that God knows from the beginning what lies ahead. He will not allow your problems to crush you. Every problem we face has a purpose. It moves us one step ahead and builds us up. Our Father watches over us day and night and He will not allow you to stand alone in your moment of difficulty.

He has a plan for you, and learning through your problems is part of that plan. God stood by me in my hour of darkness and He will do the same for you. Sometimes it would be so easy just to fold your arms, do nothing or just waste away. Other times it would be tempting to cry out to heaven and accuse God to His face. I have seen it happen many times.

Don't allow despair and temporary setbacks to water down your faith in God. Don't allow yourself to get into a "why bother" attitude. Self-pity will do you no good. It has caused many people, including Christians, to fall by the wayside and give up. Don't let your despair throw you off balance. On this pathway of faith the enemy is against us. He comes to steal, kill and destroy. The devil will do his worst for you, but God will do His best for you. Through the blood of Jesus, God's power is able to see you through all the problems which beset us in the world today.

The prison sentence I received shook me to the foundation, but it could not cause my downfall. It was my person-to-person relationship with the Almighty God that brought me through. My personal acquaintance with Him was what drew the line between failure or success and now I can move on in the power of God. To be branded a drug smuggler is a humiliating experience, and I could not have coped alone. Whatever the circumstances, I encourage you to set your eyes by faith on the Lord, keep looking to Him and continue looking until the tide turns in your favour.

God doesn't always reveal his plans and purposes, but
"we know that everything works together for good to those who love the Lord, and are called according to His purpose."

Now I am able to follow God's leading and try and work out my vision.

God can do the same with your vision and dreams, some of them far beyond anything you could imagine. Don't lose sight of them. Faith makes all things possible. Faith in God changes things no matter how hopeless they may look.

Praise the Lord.

Bible References
Found in the Text

Quotations are taken from the *The New International Version* translation of the Bible, unless otherwise stated.
AV is used for the *Authorized Version*.
All direct quotations are shown in italics. Other passages referred to are in regular text.

Chapter 2

Jesus being questioned by Annas, Caiaphas, Pilate and Herod. *John 18 and Luke 23*

Chapter 3

When you come, bring the cloak that I left with Carpus at Troas. *2 Timothy 4 v 13*

Three Hebrew boys. *Daniel 3*

Chapter 7

From the rising of the sun until the going down of the same the Lord's name is to be praised. *Psalm 113 v 3 AV*

But I tell you, do not swear at all.... Simply let your "Yes" be "Yes" and your "No" "No". *Matthew 5 v 34, 37*

Chapter 8

Weep not for me, but weep for yourselves and your children. *Luke 23 v 28 AV*

The law is slacked, and judgement doth never go forth: for

*the wicked doth compass about the righteous; therefore
wrong judgement proceedeth.* *Habakkuk 1 v 4 AV*

Chapter 10

*If only I knew where to find him; if only I could go to his
dwelling! I would state my case before him and fill my
mouth with arguments. I would find out what he would
answer me and consider what he would say. But if I go to
the east, he is not there; if I go to the west, I do not find him.
When he is at work in the north, I do not see him; when he
turns to the south, I catch no glimpse of him. But he knows
the way that I take; when he has tested me, I shall come
forth as gold.* *Job 23 vs 3 - 10*

*And we know that all things work together for good to them
that love God, to them who are the called according to his
purpose.* *Romans 8 v 28 AV*

*It is as sport to a fool to do mischief: but a man of
understanding has wisdom.* *Proverbs 10 v 23 AV*

*And these signs will accompany those who believe: In my
name they will drive out demons; they will speak in new
tongues; they will pick up snakes with their hands; and
when they drink deadly poison, it will not hurt them at all;
they will place their hands on sick people, and they will get
well.* *Mark 16 v 17*

Chapter 11

Joseph in prison. *Genesis 39; 40*

Shadrach, Meshach and Abednego. *Daniel 3*

Daniel in the lions' den. *Daniel 6*

Paul being stoned. *Acts 14 v 19*

Jesus in Gethsemane. *Matthew 26 v 36-45*

Keeping a close watch on him, they sent spies who pretended to be honest. *Luke 20 v 20*

For he shall give his angels charge over you, to keep you in all your ways. *Psalm 91 v 11 AV*

An angel rescues Peter from prison *Acts 12 v 7-10*

Chapter 12

Only rebel not ye against the Lord, neither fear ye the people of the land; for they are bread for us: their defence is departed from them, and the Lord is with us: fear them not.
Numbers 14 v 9 AV

Chapter 13

A broken and contrite heart, O God, you will not despise.
Psalm 51 v 17

If any man be in Christ he is a new creature: old things are passed away; behold, all things are become new.
2 Corinthians 5 v 17 AV

Whatsoever you do, do it heartily, as to the Lord, and not unto men; *Colossians 3 v 23 AV*

Seven evil spirits. *Matthew 12 v 45*

God moves in a mysterious way His wonders to perform.
Hymn by William Cowper, based on   *Romans 11 vs 33-36*

Many are the afflictions of the righteous, but the Lord delivereth him out of them all.   *Psalm 34 v 19 AV*

Chapter 15

Job and his friends.   *Job 2*

I will never leave you or forsake you.
Hebrews 13 v 5; Deuteronomy 31 v 6

How long, O Lord, must I cry for help, but you do not listen?   *Habakkuk 1 v 2*

Mary, Martha and Lazarus.   *John 11 v 1- 43*

When you pass through the waters, I will be with you; and when you pass through the rivers, they will not sweep over you. When you walk through the fire, you will not be burned; the flames will not set you ablaze. For I am the Lord, your God, the Holy One of Israel, your Saviour;
Isaiah 43 v 2,3

Lo, I am with you always, even to the end of the world.
Matthew 28 v 20 AV

Verily the Lord hath heard me, He hath attended to the voice of my prayer.   *Psalm 66 v 19 AV*

Chapter 16

We know that all things work together for good to them that love God, to them who are called according to his purpose.
Romans 8 v 28 AV